THE SOUTH BEACH DIET

Taste of Summer Cookbook

THE SOUTH BEACH DIET

Taste of Summer Cookbook

Arthur Agatston, MD

RODALE

© 2007 by Arthur Agatston, MD
The South Beach Diet® is a registered trademark of the SBD Trademark Limited Partnership.

Rodale books may be purchased for business or promotional use or for special sales.
For information, please write to:
Special Markets Department, Rodale Inc., 733 Third Avenue, New York, NY 10017

Printed in the United States of America
Rodale Inc. makes every effort to use acid-free ⊗, recycled paper ♲.

Book design by Carol Angstadt
Photography by Mitch Mandel
Food styling by Diane Simone Vezza
Prop styling by Francine Matalon-Degni

Photograph on the front cover is Grilled Shrimp Salad with Chile-Lime Dressing (page 124)
Photographs on pages vi–vii, xii, 44–45, 122–123, 182–183, and 233 © Getty Images

Library of Congress Cataloging-in-Publication Data

Agatston, Arthur.
    The South Beach diet taste of summer cookbook / Arthur Agatston.
        p.   cm.
    Includes index.
    ISBN-13 978–1–59486–445–2 hardcover
    ISBN-10 1–59486–445–4 hardcover
    1. Reducing diets—Recipes.   I. Title.
RM222.2.A3497   2007
641.5′63—dc22   2007001033

Distributed to the trade by Holtzbrinck Publishers

2   4   6   8   10   9   7   5   3   1   hardcover

We inspire and enable people to improve their lives and the world around them
For more of our products visit **rodalestore.com** or call 800-848-4735

To my wife, Sari,
and sons, Evan and Adam

CONTENTS

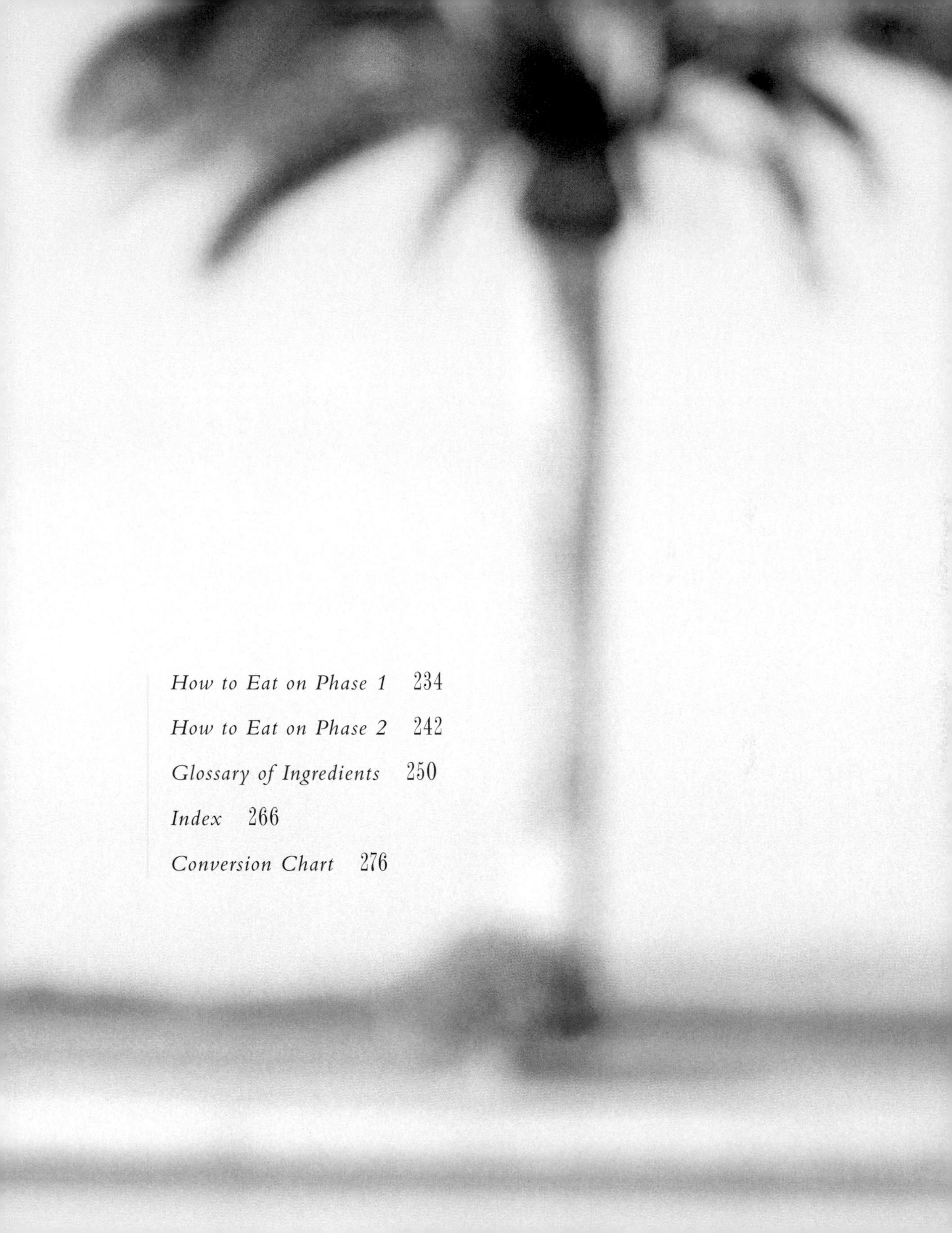

ACKNOWLEDGMENTS

Many people have helped to produce this refreshing addition to our library of South Beach Diet cookbooks. At Rodale, I would like to thank Liz Perl, Margot Schupf, and Cindy Ratzlaff for their continued support, as well as my incredible editor, Marya Dalrymple, whose fondness for grilling inspired a number of the recipes in this book.

I would also like to thank art director Carol Angstadt and photographer Mitch Mandel for their creative vision, and project editor Nancy N. Bailey, test kitchen director JoAnn Brader, food stylist Diane Simone Vezza, and prop stylist Francine Matalon-Degni for their many hours of work on the book.

In addition, my appreciation goes to Mindy Fox for overseeing the creation and development of the recipes, and to Marie Almon, my nutrition director, for her guidance.

I am also grateful to Margo Lowry of the South Beach Diet partnership for her advice, and to my publicists, Alice McGillion and Lori Ferme of Rubenstein Communications, for their energy.

And, of course, no summer meal would be as enjoyable without my wife, Sari, and my sons, Evan and Adam, to share it with. As always, I thank Sari for her great taste and keen editorial eye.

FOREWORD

I love summer. The days are bright and long, with sundown arriving well into evening. Work schedules are generally more relaxed, school is out, and vacations are just around the corner.

In Miami Beach, where I practice medicine and live with my family, summers are hot and humid with lots of brief showers. But the days are also gloriously quiet and calm, since most tourists come to South Florida "out of season." Many summers we travel as a family, perhaps taking some time away in a cooler climate. But we are always happy to come home to a relaxed, less-congested, balmy Miami Beach. For us, this is a time to invite friends over for casual grilled lunches and dinners next to the pool; a time to walk the relatively empty beaches; a time to play lots of golf, cheer for the Marlins, and enjoy other outdoor activities as a family.

During summer, I often find myself thinking just how perfectly the season captures the South Beach Diet lifestyle. Garden- and market-fresh ingredients are more available than ever. And with very little effort, they turn into bountiful salads dressed in healthy olive-oil vinaigrettes, refreshing chilled fruit or vegetable soups, and lively spice-rubbed grilled meat, poultry, and fish dishes—the very foods that, for us, are the perfect antidote to the sultry South Florida heat.

Summer is also the best time to reap the maximum health benefits of fruits and vegetables at their peak. Freshly harvested, these nutritious foods are particularly high in phytochemicals—plant-based micronutrients that act in numerous ways, including as antioxidants, to protect your health. Perhaps you've heard of *lycopene,* a member of the carotenoid family; it's found in tomatoes, papaya, and other fruits. Or *anthocyanins,* which exist in blueberries, cherries, purple grapes, plums, eggplant, and more. Or *lutein,* which is present in spinach and other dark leafy greens. Or *polyphenols,* which show up in garlic and onions and, yes, in red wine, green tea, and dark chocolate, too. These are just some of the thousands of phytochemicals that help to fight all kinds of diseases and disorders, including cancer and high blood pressure. For more information on the nutritional benefits of these and other foods, turn to the glossary, starting on page 250.

The point is, when you eat a wide variety of nutritious whole fruits and vegetables (in addition to whole grains, good fats, lean protein, and low-fat dairy), you not only improve your health but also get the greatest enjoyment from the South Beach Diet lifestyle. In fact, I've often found that the people who are most successful on the South Beach Diet are those who make a conscious effort to try new recipes and take advantage of as many food choices as possible.

As you'll see by browsing through this book, there are loads of possibilities for summertime eating. If you're a fan of burgers and hot dogs, like I am, you'll find plenty of healthy variations on these popular foods. If you like lighter fare, we've got delicious soup and salad suggestions. And, of course, no summer day would be complete without a refreshing drink (try my favorite, Iced Pom-Mojito Spritzers, page 228) or a taste of dessert (I'm partial to the Chocolate-Cherry Truffles, page 200!).

But as I've said so many times before, the foundation for truly healthy living is more than just a sound diet. Exercise is an essential component. And what better time than summer to get outside and get moving? When you combine the principles of healthy eating with a regular exercise program, you are employing the most powerful approach to shedding unwanted pounds, maintaining a healthy weight, and improving your overall well-being, while avoiding a host of health-related problems. On the next page, I give you some tips on walking, which I consider to be the ideal summertime exercise for people of all ages. Just put on some sunscreen, walk out your door, and go!

Living in Miami Beach, where cool, fresh foods and outdoor exercise are a way of life, my family has the pleasure of enjoying "summer" year-round. Now you can experience the fresh tastes of the season, just as we do, by preparing and serving the delicious, healthy recipes in this book.

ARTHUR AGATSTON, MD

Walking: The Perfect Summertime Exercise

Summer is a great time to cook, dine, *and* exercise outdoors! While any form of aerobic exercise (like swimming, hiking, or playing tennis or even softball) is excellent, walking at a brisk pace for 30 minutes a day is one of the best, and the easiest, exercises to do on a regular basis—whatever your age or ability. You can walk wherever summer takes you, whether it's on the beach, through the woods, around the block, or even around the mall on a rainy day. When time is tight, park your car farther from the office, market, or shopping center. Walking here and there for 5 to 10 minutes will quickly add up to 30 minutes. Before you get started, here are some considerations:

Build a gradual routine. Consult with your doctor before beginning any new form of exercise. Step up your walking routine gradually, over a week or two, working up to 30 minutes as you get more fit.

Walk at a brisk pace. Consider a scale of 1 to 10, with 1 being the absolute slowest speed you can walk and 10 being the fastest you can walk without losing your breath. A "brisk" walk falls into the 6 to 7 range (later, as you gradually improve, you can move into the 8 to 10 range). If you can carry on a conversation at your fastest pace, you're in good shape. If not, take it down a notch. Begin and end your walk with 5 minutes at the 3 to 4 pace, and walk at your top pace for the 20 minutes in between. Breathe normally during the walk, and take a few deep breaths before stopping.

Practice good form and posture. Walk from heel to toe, pushing off from the toes with each step. Keep your chest lifted, your abdominals consciously drawn in, and your chin parallel to the ground. You should feel an invigorating, lengthening sensation as you walk.

Add resistance exercises. For a well-rounded workout, incorporate 15 minutes of stretching and strength-enhancing resistance exercises into your exercise program at least three times a week. This will keep your muscles and joints in shape and free from injury. You may want to try Pilates, a method of body conditioning that is great for any age and fitness level.

SUMMERTIME ON THE SOUTH BEACH DIET

Summer is a great time to enjoy your South Beach Diet lifestyle. With the abundance of fresh fruits and vegetables available at this time of year, it's so easy to eat healthy. Whether you shop at a local farmers' market or supermarket or enjoy the bounty of your own garden, the foods of summer naturally suit the South Beach Diet.

Since we all like to relax during these warm months, preparing food should be laid-back and fun. The easy recipes in this book help you do just that, any night of the week, whether you're eating in or making food for a picnic, barbecue, camping trip, day at the beach, or ballgame. Imagine packing a cooler with South Beach Diet Club Sandwiches (page 51), a side of Savoy Slaw with Sesame Dressing (page 88), and fresh Summer Fruit Cocktail for dessert (page 212). Add some plastic utensils, a few napkins, and a bottle of water and you're good to go!

Burgers, hot dogs, fries, and creamy potato and egg salads are on everyone's list of summer favorites, including ours, so we've updated them—creating healthy versions that are tastier than ever. Juicy Chimichurri Burgers (page 148) are made with lean ground beef, and there are Asian Tuna Burgers (page 116) and South-of-the-Border Salmon Burgers (page 117), too. We've lightened up potato salad with a creamy yogurt dressing (page 81), and egg salad by using more egg whites than yolks (page 47). Hot dogs are dressed with a homemade tomato and pickle relish (page 158) that's sugar free and much lower in sodium than supermarket versions. For vegetarians, there are tasty Chicago-style tofu dogs (page 181), charred on the grill and topped with hot peppers, ripe tomato slices, tangy mustard, and more. You'll make delicious grilled fries using fiber-rich sweet potatoes (page 86), and refreshing Peach-Raspberry Shakes (page 230) that taste as rich as those made with ice cream. And this is just the beginning!

Along with these best-loved American summer foods, there are recipes inspired by the cuisines of warm climes around the globe. You'll find Spanish White Gazpacho (page 43), made with protein- and fiber-rich almonds; Caribbean-style drinks (pages 223 and 228); Middle Eastern grilled meatballs (page 156); and Moroccan Couscous (page 77). On hot days, you might make Summer's Bounty Greek Salad (page 66) or enjoy a simple piece of spice-rubbed chicken or fish with a side of Spanish Rice Salad with Pumpkin Seeds (page 89). For cooler days and nights, try Quick Chicken Tagine (page 134) or Southern-Style Shrimp Boil (page 96).

No matter which recipe you choose, you'll find we've used healthy and easy cooking techniques, like grilling and quick sautéing, throughout the book. You won't be toiling over a hot stove or heating up the kitchen for hours with the oven on high. And with a little advance planning, you can maximize your time outdoors and with the family. Spend some time on Sunday thinking through the meals you'd like to make during the coming week. Refer to the sample meal plans on pages 234 to 249, which combine recipes from the book with other quick-to-put-together dishes for Phases 1 and 2. If you're making Grilled Chicken Fajitas (page 143), for instance, throw on some extra chicken to use in tomorrow's lunch of Curried Chicken Salad with Peanuts (page 136); use it instead of the sautéed chicken the recipe calls for. Or add a piece of salmon to the grill for a delicious next-day supper of Grilled Salmon and Farro Salad (page 105). By thinking ahead and doing some advance preparation, you can save valuable time to relax and enjoy more summer fun.

The Phases: A Short Course

Here are the fundamentals of the South Beach Diet's three phases:

Phase 1: This is the shortest phase of the diet, lasting only 2 weeks. Phase 1 is for people who have a substantial amount of weight to lose or who experience significant cravings for sugar and refined starches. During this phase, you'll jump-start your weight loss and stabilize your blood sugar levels to minimize cravings by eating a diet rich in healthy lean protein (fish, chicken, and lean cuts of beef), vegetables, nuts, reduced-fat cheeses, eggs, low-fat dairy, and good unsaturated fats, such as extra-virgin olive oil. You'll enjoy three satisfying meals a day, plus at least two snacks, and you'll even be able to have some desserts. What you won't be eating are starches (bread, pasta, and rice) or sugar (including fruit and fruit juices). While this may be hard at first, remember that in just 2 weeks you'll be adding many of these foods back into your life. Exercise during all phases is important to your overall health and will improve your results.

Phase 2: Those people who have 10 pounds or less to lose, who don't have problems with cravings, or who simply want to improve their health can start the diet with Phase 2. If you're moving on to Phase 2 from Phase 1, you'll find that your weight will continue to drop steadily and your cravings will have subsided. You'll gradually reintroduce many of the foods that were off-limits on Phase 1, including more good carbs such as whole-grain breads, whole-wheat pasta, and brown rice, as well as whole fruits and some root vegetables (such as sweet potatoes). You'll even be able to have a glass or two of red or white wine with meals if you like. Continue on Phase 2 until you reach a weight that's healthy for you.

Phase 3: This phase begins once you reach your healthy weight. At this point, you'll fully understand how to make good food choices while maintaining your health and weight. Since your South Beach Diet lifestyle will be second nature and you'll be able to monitor your body's response to particular foods with ease, you'll find yourself naturally making the right choices. Remember, once you reach Phase 3, no food is off-limits. You can even enjoy a few bites of a decadent dessert on occasion.

How to Use This Book

Whether you're on Phase 1 or Phase 2 or have made the South Beach Diet your lifestyle, this book will provide you with plenty of great recipes to cook all summer long. By utilizing the seemingly inexhaustible variety of fresh foods available, you'll have no trouble creating healthy meals whatever the occasion. But first, let's take a look at how this book is organized.

We've divided the book into nine chapters (from energizing breakfasts to cooling drinks), each filled with fresh, light recipes that take advantage of summer's most exciting flavors. To start the day, you'll find pancakes and French toast loaded with berries and other summer fruits, as well as some surprising egg dishes and more. You'll then move on to cooling soups and healthy sandwiches, bountiful salads and side dishes, and satisfying main courses for fish and poultry lovers, meat eaters, and vegetarians alike. And naturally, we've got delicious desserts and refreshing drinks for all phases of the diet. Keep in mind that if your garden or farmers' market is overflowing with juicy tomatoes or bright zucchini and yellow squash, or if the kids are clamoring for chicken or pasta, you can simply turn to the index (page 266) to find recipes organized by main ingredient and, of course, by phase.

Whatever phase of the diet you're on, you'll have a multitude of satisfying dishes to choose from. During Phase 1, for example, you might start your day with Summer Squash Scramble with Fresh Tomato (page 17), then enjoy some reduced-fat cheese and celery sticks for a midmorning snack. For lunch, try a bowl of Garden White Bean Soup (page 46) paired with some turkey breast slices and a green salad. In the afternoon, snack on hummus and bell pepper slices. Then, for dinner, choose Grilled Tuna with Provençal Anchovy Sauce (page 108) and a side of Grilled Asparagus with Lemon Aioli (page 76). Keep in mind that on Phase 1 you can always enjoy Phase 2 burgers and sandwiches—the seasonings and sauces are so tasty, you'll have no trouble skipping the bun and savoring the filling on its own. Of course, all healthy eaters can enjoy Phase 1 recipes.

With each recipe, we've also provided prep and cook times. When you're making several dishes for a meal, you can often prepare one while another is cooking. This will help reduce your time in the kitchen. For example, while you're marinating the lamb cubes for Spicy Lamb Kebabs with Cucumber-Mint Yogurt (page 169), you can prepare a side dish of Grilled Fennel with Mixed Olives (page 83) or toss together a simple salad. Remember, you can grill meats and fish for sandwiches a day or two ahead, mix drinks and make slaws in advance, and get a head start on baked goods, frozen desserts, and fruit salads.

Since many of the recipes are adaptable, you can alter them to fit what's freshest at the market. If the tuna looks fresher than the salmon, for example, try swapping one for the other. If the peaches look better than the nectarines, use them instead. And as summer wanes, you can often substitute fall and winter produce so that you can enjoy many of the recipes year-round. We've also provided a guide for preserving fresh summer fruits and vegetables for use in cooler months (see "Extending the South Beach Summer," page 10).

Summer Food Safety

Food safety should always be at the top of your mind, especially when outside temperatures soar. You can avoid many common food-related health problems by taking the following precautions: Wash your hands thoroughly with hot soapy water before, during, and after handling food. Soak fruits, vegetables, and greens for 2 minutes, then rinse well under running water to remove dirt and other contaminants. Thaw frozen meats in the microwave or the refrigerator, not at room temperature. When storing raw meats in the refrigerator, keep them well sealed and on the bottom shelf to prevent juices from dripping onto other foods. Keep cutting boards used for raw meat separate from those used for fruits and vegetables or cooked meats to avoid cross-contamination, and wash them thoroughly after each use. Pack food for travel, picnics, and barbecues in well-insulated coolers or insulated bags with plenty of ice. Instead of transporting coolers in the trunk, place them in the backseat of your air-conditioned car. When grilling or picnicking, choose a shaded spot for outdoor buffet foods and coolers and avoid letting prepared foods sit out for more than 1 hour in hot weather. See "Great Grilling on the South Beach Diet" (page 9) for more safety tips.

Healthy Eating All Summer Long

The recipes in this book have a few key things in common: They are diverse and delicious, for starters! And they're composed of slowly digested, nutrient-dense, fiber-rich foods like whole fruits, vegetables, and whole grains, as well as good fats, lean protein, and low-fat dairy. These types of foods help keep your blood sugar stable, and they promote satiety—the feeling of fullness that signals you are no longer hungry. This is important because eating foods that leave you feeling satisfied can help lead to weight loss success.

Eating the right foods can also improve your health in numerous other ways. Let's start with fruits and vegetables. You may have heard of something called the ORAC (Oxygen Radical Absorbance Capacity) scale, which measures the total antioxidant potency of foods. (Antioxidants are what protect you from free radicals, naturally occurring molecules that can damage cells and eventually cause disease if left unchecked.) Summer fruits that rank high on the ORAC scale include blueberries, blackberries, raspberries, strawberries, plums, red grapes, and cherries. You'll enjoy them in such recipes as Grilled Pork and Plum Salad with Almond Gremolata (page 167) and Strawberry-Blueberry Crunch (page 209). In the vegetable category, the season's antioxidant all-stars include kale, garlic, spinach, yellow squash, broccoli, red bell peppers, and eggplant. Try these in Curried Summer Squash Soup (page 36), Southern-Style Greens (page 85), and other great recipes.

Like fruits and vegetables, whole grains and legumes also contain antioxidant-rich phytochemicals as well as good amounts of fiber. In this book, we use a wide variety of beans and grains, including farro and wheat berries, which may be new to you. We also use nuts and seeds (in moderation) because they provide high-quality plant protein and also good monounsaturated and polyunsaturated fats. Some, like pistachios, almonds, sunflower seeds, pine nuts, and flaxseeds, are particularly high in plant sterols, which (along with other monounsaturated fats like olive oil and canola oil) can help reduce "bad" LDL cholesterol. And, of course, the book is full of recipes for omega-3-rich fish and shellfish and lean poultry and meat dishes. Vegetarians will also be pleased to find a good selection of recipes featuring tempeh, tofu, beans, and whole grains.

Making the Most of Summer's Herbs

Fantastic flavor enhancers for healthy summer dishes, herbs can be used in everything from soups and salads to sauces and even desserts! The tips below, on pages 11 and 12, and in the glossary, on pages 256 and 257, will guide you.

Substitute dried herbs for fresh, and vice versa. Substitutions can be made in many of the recipes in this book using a simple 3 (fresh herb) to 1 (dried herb) ratio. For example, if a recipe calls for 1 tablespoon (3 teaspoons) fresh rosemary, use 1 teaspoon dried.

Purchase wisely. When purchasing fresh herbs, look for bright leaves with few blemishes and a vibrant fresh scent.

Store fresh herbs to last. Wrap fresh herbs loosely in barely dampened paper towels, place in a resealable plastic bag with the air pressed out (leaving a small opening), and keep in the refrigerator produce drawer for 3 to 5 days. You can also store fresh herbs like basil, parsley, and cilantro bouquet style. Place stems in a glass with a few inches of cool water. Keep bouquets on a countertop in a cool area, away from sunlight and heat.

Grow your own. Always have fresh herbs at your fingertips (and reduce grocery bills!) by growing them in your garden or on a balcony, windowsill, or counter. Buy potted herbs at your local farmers' market or nursery, where you can also get specific growing tips.

Make fresh herb vinegars. Clean fresh herbs and pat them dry. Place in a small plastic or glass container. Cover the herbs with cider vinegar, red or white wine vinegar, or rice wine vinegar. Seal and refrigerate for 2 weeks; strain and discard the herbs. Use herb vinegars in salads and marinades. If the herb flavor is too strong, add more vinegar to dilute.

Brew fresh herb teas. Simmer 8 to 10 tablespoons (or more to taste) of a fresh herb such as peppermint, chamomile, lemon balm, or lemongrass in 4 cups water for 15 minutes. Strain and refrigerate for iced tea or serve hot. You can enhance herb teas by adding citrus peel or fennel seeds to the simmering water.

But choosing the right foods is only one part of the success equation. You also need to get the proper nutrients at regular intervals throughout the day. This means starting with a healthy breakfast, which provides you with the energy you need to embark on the day ahead. When you feel hungry again, a couple of hours later, you'll want to have a protein or high-fiber snack. In fact, having at least two healthy snacks a day keeps you energized and sated between meals. Examples of great summer snacks include nonfat or low-fat plain yogurt with fresh berries (page 18); chilled gazpacho (page 42); Mango Lassi (page 218); and green or yellow beans tossed with a little extra-virgin olive oil and your favorite chopped fresh herb. Take snacks like these to work or bring them along while you're enjoying outdoor activities like biking, hiking, and boating.

For lunch, you'll refuel with a chilled soup, perhaps, followed by a salad or a sandwich like Pan Bagnat (page 48), made with canned tuna, green beans, boiled eggs, and fresh tomatoes (it can be prepared up to a day in advance). For dinner, there are plenty of easy-to-prepare dishes like Grilled Pork Tenderloin with Peach-Lime Salsa (page 150), which can be served at room temperature, buffet style, for family or guests to enjoy. And, of course, South Beach dieters can always enjoy dessert in moderation. On Phase 1, try Iced Vanilla Coffee Milk (page 203) or Creamy Lemon-Vanilla Ricotta Soufflés (page 197). Phase 2 will bring refreshing Raspberry Ices (page 204) and other fruit desserts. And by Phase 3, you'll be able to enjoy more elaborate treats like our Floating Caribbean Islands (page 208).

With these great recipes and others like them (see the sample meal plans on pages 234 to 249 for more tempting ideas), you'll find it easy to live your South Beach Diet lifestyle all summer long. You'll even notice that when you eat well, you exercise better, and vice versa. Of course, there will be parties and other social events to attend during the summer, but this shouldn't throw you off track. By having a healthy snack before you go out, keeping alcohol intake to a minimum (you can enjoy a glass or two of red or white wine with food on Phases 2 and 3), and reaching for the crudités instead of the chips and crackers, you'll be well set to enjoy any occasion.

Great Grilling on the South Beach Diet

As many of the recipes in this book show, grilling is a favorite summer cooking technique when it comes to preparing tasty, healthy, quick, and easy recipes. From Grilled Steak with Texas Mop Sauce (page 163) and Pork Pinchos with Shredded Cabbage Salad (page 160) to Mixed Seafood Kebabs with Parsley-Garlic Sauce (page 109), Grilled Tempeh Burgers with Horseradish Aioli (page 188), Grilled Chipotle Onion Rings (page 84), and even grilled pizzas (pages 175 to 177), a wide selection of flavorful grilled dishes awaits you.

Moreover, grilling isn't just an outdoor activity anymore. Now indoor grill pans make grilling easy for anyone, anytime, whether you live in the country or city, whether it's summer or winter, raining or snowing. The recipes in this book assume the use of an outdoor gas grill or grill pan with regard to temperature setting and cooking times, but you can use charcoal, if you prefer.

Here are some basic grilling tips:

• When using fat-free cooking spray (which cuts the need for extra oils), coat the grill *before* igniting or heating. Never spray a lit outdoor grill or a grill pan with a lit flame or hot burner underneath!

• Long-handled tongs and basting brushes, bent-handled spatulas, and heat-resistant mitts are helpful for protecting your hands while grilling. If mitts become even slightly wet, dry them completely before using to avoid steam burns.

• An instant-read thermometer will help ensure that meats are cooked to the safest temperatures. We suggest cooking burgers to 160°F and pork roasts to 150°F to 155°F.

• Perforated grill racks, grilling baskets, and fish baskets can be used to grill small vegetables, delicate fish fillets, shellfish, and more, ensuring that the food won't slip through the grates.

• Before skewering and grilling food, soak wooden skewers in water for 30 minutes to keep them from burning. Use mitts to handle metal skewers, which quickly become hot once in use.

- Have your ingredients and grilling tools organized and in place before grilling to avoid leaving the grill unattended once you're cooking. Be sure to have a clean plate or platter handy to place cooked foods on as they come off the grill. If you plan to use grilling woods like those mentioned on the opposite page, you'll want to start the grill early enough to get the woods smoking.

- Trim excess fat from steaks and pork cuts. This prevents flare-ups and charring and makes cleaning the grill easier.

- Clean outdoor grills with a wire grill brush before and after each use (and while the grill is hot) so that food bits don't cool and dry onto the grates. Do not use a wire brush on grill pans, which should be cleaned with a gentle-scrub sponge, hot water, and soap.

Extending the South Beach Summer

As the long, hot summer days begin to wane, there's no need to give up the healthy foods and quick-cooking techniques you've been enjoying. All of the grilling recipes in this book can be made indoors, and while some produce may not be at its best in cooler months, many fruits and vegetables are now available year-round. When they're not, substitute. You'll find many of the recipes in this book work just as well with fall and winter produce. For example, you can enjoy diced apples or pears in place of apricots in Easy Walnut Muesli with Fresh Apricots (page 21) or use sliced oranges in place of strawberries in Sweet Strawberries with Greek-Style Yogurt and Almonds (page 18). And you'll also discover that many of the dishes we serve chilled or at room temperature heat up very well: Try Indian Spiced Chilled Tomato Soup (page 35), Curried Summer Squash Soup (page 36), and Poached Chicken, Zucchini, and Wheat Berry Salad (page 65) warm in cooler months.

But perhaps the best way to preserve summer's bounty is to freeze berries, tomatoes, and other fruits and vegetables, as well as fresh herbs, at the height of the season. A few baking sheets and plenty of resealable plastic bags specifically designed for freezing are all you'll need. Be sure to press out any air before sealing, and label and date the bags using a permanent marker. Keeping

Flavor Enhancers for Grilled Foods

Healthy and quick to cook, fish and shellfish and lean cuts of meat (like bone-less, skinless chicken breast, pork loin, lean steaks and ground beef, and turkey cutlets) are delicious when prepared on the grill. And with a little help from a variety of flavorful grilling woods and herbs and/or dry rubs, you can get great taste while using less fat and salt. Here are some ideas you can try throughout the summer or at any time of the year:

Grilling woods: Hardwoods like mesquite, hickory, cherry, cedar, and apple (which are commonly sold in chips, chunks, and planks) add a fantastic smoky flavor to all kinds of grilled foods, from steaks to vegetables. Use them on outdoor gas or charcoal grills only (not with indoor grill pans), following the instructions that come with the woods and your particular grill. You can buy woods for grilling, as well as convenient smoker boxes, from many Internet sources.

Grilling herbs: Fresh herbs make surprisingly useful and flavorful grilling "tools." Try using sturdy rosemary sprigs as skewers for shrimp or scallops. Try fresh dill or fennel with whole trout, tying the herbs in place around the fish with kitchen twine. Or tie a bouquet of fresh herbs together to make a handy brush to spread sauces or marinades onto foods as you grill.

Dry rubs: Mixing together a few pantry ingredients creates endless variations for dry rubs (so called because they use dried herbs and spices and are literally rubbed onto raw meats, poultry, and fish before cooking). While it's true that many dry rubs include sugar, there are plenty of flavor-packed versions that don't. You can make a Jamaican jerk rub, for instance, by com-bining 1 tablespoon onion powder, 1 tablespoon dried thyme, 2 teaspoons ground allspice, 2 teaspoons ground ginger, 2 teaspoons freshly ground black pepper, 2 teaspoons ground cinnamon, ½ teaspoon ground nutmeg, ¼ tea-spoon salt, and cayenne pepper to taste. Or create a Mediterranean-style rub with crushed fennel seeds, paprika, garlic powder, freshly ground black pep-per, salt, and ground dried lemon peel. Pick your favorite herbs and spices and experiment.

an inventory of the freezer contents handy will help remind you what's available. Here are some freezing tips:

Freezing vegetables: Prepare vegetables for freezing by cutting or shredding them to the desired size, briefly steaming or boiling them for 2 to 3 minutes (don't cook through), then plunging them into a bowl of ice water to stop the cooking. Drain and pat dry before freezing. This method helps vegetables retain their flavor, texture, and color through the freezing and thawing processes. Great summer veggies to freeze include green and yellow beans, broccoli, peas, bell peppers (which you can choose to boil briefly or not), summer squash, and zucchini. Tomatoes can be frozen whole (peeled or unpeeled) or cooked into sauces and then frozen; see the recipe for quick fresh tomato sauce, below. Label and date bags before freezing.

Freezing fruits: Select berries and other fruits when they are ripe but not too soft. Place the washed and gently dried fruits in single layers on baking sheets and place the sheets in the freezer until the fruit is frozen solid. Pack the frozen fruits into resealable bags, label, and date. When freezing peaches, plums, nectarines, apricots, and cherries, pit them first; for seedless grapes, remove the stems first. Melons can be seeded, cubed, and frozen.

Freezing herbs: Freezing is the best way to preserve the delicate flavor of soft-leaved herbs such as tarragon, chives, sage, and dill. Using tongs to hold a few stems at a time, dip the herbs into a pot of boiling water for a few seconds, then immediately transfer to a bowl of ice water. Dry between layers of paper towels, then place the herbs on wax or parchment paper, in single layers. Roll up the paper, press down to flatten, and store in a labeled, dated resealable plastic bag. You do not need to unroll the entire roll in order to use frozen herbs.

Another great way to avoid wasting an overabundance of summer produce is to make and freeze delicious sauces and compotes. Here are a few easy ideas to try:

Quick fresh tomato sauce: Place 2½ pounds plum tomatoes in a large saucepan of lightly salted boiling water for 45 seconds. Drain, cool, and slip the skins off; discard the skins. Slice the tomatoes and discard the seeds;

roughly chop. In a large saucepan over medium heat, cook 2 minced garlic cloves in 1 tablespoon extra-virgin olive oil, stirring, for 30 seconds. Add the tomatoes and a pinch of salt and pepper. Cook at a high simmer, stirring occasionally, for 12 to 15 minutes. Adjust the seasoning, adding red pepper flakes or dried herbs, such as oregano and basil, if desired. Cool completely, and freeze in resealable bags or plastic containers (leaving a 1½-inch space at the top for sauce to expand into as it freezes). Double the recipe if desired.

Fresh herb pestos: Lightly toast ⅓ cup walnuts, almonds, or pine nuts in a 275°F oven for about 10 minutes. In a food processor, combine the leaves of 1 large bunch of fresh basil, cilantro, or parsley (or a combination) with 1 peeled garlic clove and the toasted nuts; process for 25 seconds. With the machine running, add ¼ cup extra-virgin olive oil in a slow, steady stream. Transfer to a bowl and stir in ¼ cup freshly grated Parmesan cheese, 2 teaspoons lemon juice, and salt to taste. Freeze in plastic containers (as in the tomato sauce recipe above). You can use arugula instead of herbs, if you prefer.

Easy fruit compotes: In a small saucepan over medium-low heat, bring to a boil 1 pound blackberries, blueberries, strawberries, pitted cherries, or pitted and diced apricots, peaches, nectarines, or plums (or a combination of any of these) along with 1 teaspoon grated lemon or orange zest and 1 tablespoon granular sugar substitute. Cook, stirring occasionally, until the fruit has softened, about 5 minutes. Remove from the heat, adjust the sweetener if necessary, and cool completely before freezing, as in the quick tomato sauce recipe above.

Savor the Taste of Summer Year-Round

The joys of summer don't have to end when the days get shorter. We encourage you to follow the healthy eating principles you'll learn from this book throughout the year. Continue choosing and cooking with the freshest, healthiest ingredients available, maintain your regular exercise routine, and enjoy life with family and friends to the fullest. Remember, summer isn't just a season; it's a sunny year-round state of mind!

BREEZY BREAKFASTS

There's no better way to start a summer day—and every day—than with a good breakfast. Eating a protein- and fiber-rich meal in the morning gives you a boost of energy, improves concentration, memory, and mood, and sets you on track to eat right all day long. A nutritious breakfast also helps keep your blood sugar stable, which reduces cravings later in the day.

The pages ahead are filled with satisfying breakfast options for every day of the week. Take a Blackberry-Banana Breakfast Smoothie along to work. On more leisurely mornings, try Poached Eggs with Cherry Tomatoes and Scallions or Whole-Grain Nectarine Pancakes. The Smoked Salmon and Cream Cheese "Breakwich" is a great protein choice that's also a nice change of pace from typical morning fare. And juicy, nutritious summer fruits abound, paired with creamy Greek-style yogurt, stuffed between layers of piping-hot French toast, and folded into freshly baked muffins.

◄ *Farmer's Cheese Pancakes with Summer Fruits (page 16)*

Farmer's Cheese Pancakes with Summer Fruits

PREP TIME: 5 minutes   **COOK TIME:** 25 minutes

These delicate pancakes can be served flat or filled with the topping and rolled up.
Use an 8-inch skillet or omelet pan to make them. The creamy, semisoft version of
farmer's cheese is best here; it can be found in the dairy section of most supermarkets.

Topping

- 2 medium peaches, sliced (1 cup)
- ¼ cup water
- 2 tablespoons granular sugar substitute
- 1 teaspoon fresh lemon juice
- ¼ cup raspberries

Pancakes

- 6 large eggs, lightly beaten
- 1 cup semisoft farmer's cheese
- 2 teaspoons granular sugar substitute

Heat the oven to 200°F.

For the topping: In a small saucepan, combine peaches, water, and sugar substitute; bring to a boil over medium heat. Reduce the heat to low and simmer until peaches are soft, about 10 minutes. Remove from the heat and stir in lemon juice. Gently stir in raspberries; set aside and keep warm.

While the topping is cooking, make the pancakes: In a large bowl, whisk together eggs, ⅔ cup of the cheese, and sugar substitute.

Lightly coat an 8-inch nonstick skillet with cooking spray and heat over medium heat. Spoon ¼ cup of the batter into the pan and cook until pancake is set and edges are starting to turn golden, about 2 minutes. Loosen with a rubber spatula and flip; cook 1 minute more. Transfer pancake to a heatproof platter and place in the oven to keep warm. Repeat for remaining pancakes.

Divide pancakes among 4 plates. Spoon peach-raspberry topping over pancakes and dollop with remaining cheese. Serve warm.

Makes 4 (2-pancake) servings

NUTRITION AT A GLANCE

Per serving with fruit: 230 calories, 12 g fat, 5 g saturated fat, 19 g protein, 8 g carbohydrate, 1 g fiber, 340 mg sodium

Per serving without fruit: 206 calories, 12 g fat, 5 g saturated fat, 19 g protein, 2 g carbohydrate, 0 g fiber, 340 mg sodium

Summer Squash Scramble with Fresh Tomato

PREP TIME: 15 minutes   **COOK TIME:** 10 minutes

Zucchini, pattypan, yellow straightneck, and crookneck are just a few of the many summer squash varieties that fill the summer garden. Try any type you like for this recipe. You can also use your favorite fresh herb in place of the chives. This recipe can easily be doubled for four hungry eaters.

- 3 large eggs
- 1 teaspoon chopped chives
- ¼ teaspoon salt
- ⅛ teaspoon freshly ground black pepper
- 2 teaspoons canola oil
- 1 small yellow summer squash, halved and thinly sliced into half-moons
- ½ small onion, finely chopped
- 1 medium tomato, finely chopped

In a small bowl, beat eggs, chives, salt, and pepper until well combined.

In a medium nonstick skillet, heat oil over medium heat. Add squash and onion; cook, stirring occasionally, until softened and starting to brown, about 8 minutes.

Add egg mixture to the skillet and cook, stirring frequently, until eggs are set, about 2 minutes. Spoon eggs onto 2 plates and sprinkle with tomato. Serve warm.

Makes 2 servings

NUTRITION AT A GLANCE
Per serving: 180 calories, 12 g fat, 2.5 g saturated fat, 11 g protein, 8 g carbohydrate, 2 g fiber, 390 mg sodium

Sweet Strawberries with Greek-Style Yogurt and Almonds

PREP TIME: 5 minutes   COOK TIME: 12 minutes

Greek-style yogurt is strained for several hours before it is packaged, reducing its water content and resulting in a rich, creamy product. It's especially delicious when enjoyed with nuts and fresh fruit. This recipe also makes a satisfying snack, if you want to try it later in the day.

- ½ cup sliced almonds
- 3 cups nonfat or low-fat Greek-style plain yogurt
- 3 cups sliced strawberries

Heat the oven to 275°F. Spread almonds on a baking sheet and bake until fragrant and lightly browned, 10 to 12 minutes.

Divide yogurt evenly among 4 bowls. Top each serving with ¾ cup strawberries and 2 tablespoons almonds.

Makes 4 (1½-cup) servings

NUTRITION AT A GLANCE
Per serving: 190 calories, 7 g fat, 0.5 g saturated fat, 11 g protein, 26 g carbohydrate, 4 g fiber, 105 mg sodium

Blueberry-Almond Bran Muffins

PREP TIME: 10 minutes   **COOK TIME:** 25 minutes

A small amount of white flour, combined with whole-grain pastry flour and wheat bran, gives these muffins a lighter texture. To make them out of season, use frozen (unthawed) blueberries and fold them right into the batter. You can even freeze your own berries to use in later months. See page 12 for instructions.

1 cup whole-grain pastry flour	¼ teaspoon salt
1 cup wheat bran	1¼ cups 1% or fat-free buttermilk
½ cup all-purpose white flour	2 large eggs, lightly beaten
2 tablespoons granular sugar substitute	¼ cup canola oil
1½ teaspoons ground cinnamon	1½ teaspoons vanilla extract
1¼ teaspoons baking soda	1¼ cups blueberries
¼ teaspoon freshly ground nutmeg	⅓ cup sliced almonds

Heat the oven to 350°F. Lightly coat a 12-cup muffin tin with cooking spray.

In a large bowl, combine pastry flour, bran, white flour, sugar substitute, cinnamon, baking soda, nutmeg, and salt.

In a medium bowl, whisk together buttermilk, eggs, oil, and vanilla. Make a well in the center of the dry ingredients. Add wet ingredients to dry and mix just to combine; do not overmix.

Gently fold blueberries into batter. Divide batter evenly among muffin cups. Top with almonds and gently press them into batter. Bake muffins for 25 minutes, or until a tester inserted in the center comes out clean. Cool in the pan for 5 minutes and then remove to a rack to finish cooling.

Makes 12 servings

NUTRITION AT A GLANCE
Per serving: 150 calories, 8 g fat, 1 g saturated fat, 5 g protein, 17 g carbohydrate, 5 g fiber, 200 mg sodium

Easy Walnut Muesli with Fresh Apricots

PREP TIME: 5 minutes   **COOK TIME:** 12 minutes

Popular for breakfast in Switzerland and Germany, muesli is easy to make at home. It's delicious with the addition of golden, fresh apricots—a summertime treat that offers loads of beta-carotene and fiber. In cooler months, use diced apples or pears instead. You can store muesli in a covered container in the refrigerator for up to 2 weeks.

Muesli

- 1 cup chopped walnuts
- 1½ cups rolled oats
- ½ cup wheat germ
- ¼ cup pumpkin seeds
- ¼ cup sunflower seeds

Toppings

- 2 tablespoons ground flaxseed
- 8 fresh apricots, sliced (2 cups)
- 2 cups 1% or fat-free milk

For the muesli: Heat the oven to 275°F. Spread walnuts on a baking sheet and bake until fragrant and lightly browned, about 12 minutes. In a large bowl, combine walnuts, oats, wheat germ, pumpkin seeds, and sunflower seeds.

For each serving, place ½ cup muesli in a cereal bowl. Top each with ¾ teaspoon flaxseed and ¼ cup apricots. Add ¼ cup milk and serve.

Makes 8 (½-cup) servings

NUTRITION AT A GLANCE
Per serving: 264 calories, 15 g fat, 1.5 g saturated fat, 11 g protein, 25 g carbohydrate, 5 g fiber, 28 mg sodium

Greet-the-Sun Breakfast Pizzas

PREP TIME: 10 minutes   **COOK TIME:** 20 minutes

Pizza for breakfast? Why not? It's especially tasty when topped with a sunny-side-up egg and veggies. Quarter or halve the recipe for just one or two pizzas and try shredded part-skim mozzarella instead of feta, if you like.

- 5 teaspoons extra-virgin olive oil
- 4 ounces packed spinach (4 cups)
- 2 (6-inch) whole-grain pitas, halved horizontally
- 2 large plum tomatoes, thinly sliced
- 4 large eggs
- ¼ teaspoon salt
- ¼ teaspoon freshly ground black pepper
- 2 ounces reduced-fat feta cheese, crumbled (⅓ cup)

Heat the oven to 450°F.

In a large nonstick skillet, heat 1 teaspoon of the oil over medium heat. Add spinach, in batches if necessary, and cook until wilted, 2 to 3 minutes.

Brush inside of each pita round with 1 teaspoon oil. Place pita rounds, oiled side up, on a large baking sheet and bake until starting to brown, about 5 minutes. Remove from the oven.

Divide tomatoes and spinach evenly among pita halves, leaving an empty space in the center of each for an egg. Crack 1 egg into the center of each pita. Sprinkle with salt and pepper, return to the oven, and bake until yolks are lightly set, 8 to 10 minutes. Sprinkle with cheese and continue baking until cheese has softened, about 2 minutes more. Serve warm.

Makes 4 servings

NUTRITION AT A GLANCE
Per serving: 250 calories, 13 g fat, 3.5 g saturated fat, 13 g protein, 21 g carbohydrate, 3 g fiber, 500 mg sodium

Sweet Potato and Turkey Hash

PREP TIME: 20 minutes   **COOK TIME:** 12 minutes

Fiber-rich sweet potatoes paired with bright bell pepper and garden-fresh scallions make a healthy hash that's terrific with scrambled or poached eggs at any time of year.

- 2 teaspoons extra-virgin olive oil
- 1 small (8-ounce) sweet potato, peeled and finely chopped
- 1 small red bell pepper, finely chopped
- 2 scallions, thinly sliced
- 2 tablespoons water
- ¼ teaspoon salt
- ⅛ teaspoon freshly ground black pepper
- ⅛ teaspoon dried thyme
- ½ pound cooked skinless roast turkey breast, cut into ¼-inch cubes (1 cup)
- 2 tablespoons reduced-fat sour cream

In a large nonstick skillet, heat oil over medium heat. Add sweet potato and cook, stirring occasionally, until lightly browned and beginning to soften, about 5 minutes. Add bell pepper, scallions, water, salt, black pepper, and thyme; cook until bell pepper and scallions are softened, about 5 minutes. Stir in turkey and cook until heated through, about 2 minutes. Remove from the heat and stir in sour cream. Serve warm.

Makes 4 (½-cup) servings

NUTRITION AT A GLANCE
Per serving: 120 calories, 4.5 g fat, 1.5 g saturated fat, 12 g protein, 9 g carbohydrate, 2 g fiber, 190 mg sodium

Whole-Grain Nectarine Pancakes

PREP TIME: 10 minutes   COOK TIME: 20 minutes

A great source of fiber and B vitamins, whole-grain pastry flour makes fantastic pancakes. These are sweet and light and can be topped with peaches, plums, or berries if you prefer. Keep whole-grain flours refrigerated (or frozen) to prevent their natural oils from turning rancid.

1 cup whole-grain pastry flour	¼ cup trans-fat-free margarine, melted, plus 1 tablespoon unmelted
3 teaspoons granular sugar substitute	
1 teaspoon baking soda	1 to 2 medium nectarines, sliced (1 cup)
1 cup 1% or fat-free buttermilk	¼ teaspoon ground cinnamon
2 large eggs, lightly beaten	

Heat the oven to 200°F.

In a large bowl, combine flour, 2 teaspoons of the sugar substitute, and baking soda.

In a medium bowl, whisk together buttermilk, eggs, and melted margarine. Make a well in the center of the dry ingredients. Add wet ingredients to dry and mix just to combine; do not overmix.

Coat a large nonstick skillet or griddle with cooking spray and heat over medium heat until hot enough to cause drops of water to scatter over the surface, about 3 minutes. Working in batches if necessary, spoon a heaping tablespoon of batter onto the griddle to form a 3-inch pancake (you will be making 16 pancakes). Cook pancakes until golden brown, about 2 minutes per side. Transfer to a heatproof platter and place in the oven to keep warm until ready to serve.

In a medium nonstick skillet, heat remaining 1 tablespoon margarine over medium heat until melted. Add nectarines, cinnamon, and remaining 1 teaspoon sugar substitute. Cook, stirring occasionally, until nectarines are soft and golden, about 5 minutes. Remove pancakes from the oven and divide among 4 plates. Spoon nectarine slices over pancakes and serve.

Makes 4 (4-pancake) servings

NUTRITION AT A GLANCE
Per serving: 290 calories, 15 g fat, 4.5 g saturated fat, 9 g protein, 30 g carbohydrate, 3 g fiber, 490 mg sodium

Blackberry-Banana Breakfast Smoothies

PREP TIME: 10 minutes

Wheat germ adds protein, fiber, thiamin, and vitamin E to this fruit-packed smoothie. If your berries are very tart, add the sugar substitute.

- 2 small bananas, quartered (1½ cups)
- 1 cup blackberries, plus extra for garnish (optional)
- 1½ cups nonfat or low-fat plain yogurt
- 1 tablespoon granular sugar substitute (optional)
- 1 tablespoon wheat germ
- 4 ice cubes

In a blender, combine bananas and blackberries; purée until smooth. Add yogurt, sugar substitute, if using, wheat germ, and ice cubes; blend until smooth, about 1 minute. Pour into 4 (10-ounce) glasses, garnish with whole blackberries, if using, and serve.

Makes 4 (1-cup) servings

NUTRITION AT A GLANCE
Per serving: 100 calories, 0.5 g fat, 0 g saturated fat, 5 g protein, 21 g carbohydrate, 3 g fiber, 50 mg sodium

Poached Eggs with Cherry Tomatoes and Scallions

PREP TIME: 5 minutes   **COOK TIME:** 10 minutes

This lovely dish confirms the fact that simple recipes are often the most delicious, especially at the height of summer, when tomatoes are at their best. For a change of pace, use cherry tomatoes along with other small varieties, like grape or currant (which are extra sweet), or a combination of yellow and red pear tomatoes, which are also called "teardrop."

1 tablespoon extra-virgin olive oil

2 scallions, thinly sliced

8 ounces cherry tomatoes, halved (1¼ cups)

⅛ teaspoon salt

2 teaspoons white vinegar

2 large eggs

In a small nonstick skillet, heat oil over medium heat. Add scallions and cook until fragrant and beginning to soften, about 2 minutes. Add tomatoes and salt; cook, stirring occasionally, until tomatoes have softened and given off some of their juices, about 3 minutes. Remove the pan from the heat, cover, and keep warm.

    Bring a large saucepan of water to a boil; add vinegar. Crack 1 egg into a cup. Gently slide egg into the water. Repeat with remaining egg, using a slotted spoon to keep eggs separated from each other, if necessary. Cook at a simmer until yolks are lightly set, 3 to 4 minutes.

    Divide tomato-scallion mixture between 2 shallow bowls. Top each with an egg. Spoon any remaining liquid from the tomato mixture over the eggs. Serve warm.

Makes 2 servings

NUTRITION AT A GLANCE
Per serving: 160 calories, 12 g fat, 2.5 g saturated fat, 7 g protein, 7 g carbohydrate, 2 g fiber, 220 mg sodium

Three Berry-Stuffed French Toast

PREP TIME: 10 minutes   **COOK TIME:** 10 minutes

Blackberries, blueberries, and raspberries—bursting with juicy flavor—make a perfect French toast stuffing when paired with farmer's cheese. You could use 1%, 2%, or fat-free cottage cheese instead of farmer's cheese, if you prefer.

⅓   cup blackberries

⅓   cup blueberries

⅓   cup raspberries

⅔   cup semisoft farmer's cheese

1   tablespoon granular sugar substitute

8   slices whole-grain sandwich bread

3   large eggs

¼   cup 1% milk

¼   teaspoon ground cinnamon

In a medium bowl, combine blackberries, blueberries, raspberries, cheese, and sugar substitute. Using a fork, mash together lightly. Lay 4 slices of the bread on a work surface. Spread berry mixture evenly on slices and top with remaining bread slices to form 4 sandwiches. Lightly press around the edges to seal.

In a shallow dish, beat eggs with milk and cinnamon. Dip both sides of sandwiches into egg mixture, allow excess to drip off, and place sandwiches on a platter.

Lightly coat a nonstick skillet or griddle with cooking spray and heat over medium heat. Cook French toast in two batches until golden brown, about 2 minutes per side. Serve warm.

Makes 4 servings

NUTRITION AT A GLANCE
Per serving: 280 calories, 9 g fat, 3.5 g saturated fat, 17 g protein, 30 g carbohydrate, 5 g fiber, 470 mg sodium

Smoked Salmon and Cream Cheese "Breakwiches"

PREP TIME: 10 minutes   **COOK TIME:** 10 minutes

They might be called sandwiches at any other time of day, but our warm and creamy toasted smoked salmon breakwiches are especially nice in the morning.

    8 slices thin-sliced whole-grain bread
    2 ounces reduced-fat cream cheese (¼ cup)
    6 ounces thinly sliced smoked salmon
    2 tablespoons chopped chives
       Freshly ground black pepper
    4 teaspoons trans-fat-free margarine

Lay bread on a work surface; spread each slice with 1 tablespoon of the cream cheese. Divide smoked salmon among 4 of the slices. Sprinkle salmon evenly with chives and pepper. Top with remaining bread slices to make 4 sandwiches.

In a large nonstick skillet, heat 2 teaspoons of the margarine over medium heat. Add 2 sandwiches, weight down with a heavy pan, and cook until golden brown, about 2 minutes per side. Repeat with remaining margarine and sandwiches. Cut sandwiches in half and serve warm.

Makes 4 servings

NUTRITION AT A GLANCE
Per serving: 240 calories, 11 g fat, 4.5 g saturated fat, 19 g protein, 18 g carbohydrate, 5 g fiber, 810 mg sodium

COOL SOUPS AND SANDWICHES

Summer soups take advantage of the best vegetables available, combining them with vibrant herbs and spices. Served chilled on hot afternoons or warm on cooler evenings, soup can be a satisfying start to a meal or act as the main course. In this chapter, grilled shrimp and fresh dill top a refreshing cucumber soup; heirloom tomatoes make a special gazpacho that's filled with bright flavors; and fiber-rich white beans are puréed with garden-fresh greens.

When you're looking for casual fare that can be toted to the beach, taken to the ballgame, or packed for summer travel, a good sandwich can't be beat. Try chipotle-rubbed steak rolled up with lettuce and tomatoes in a tasty wrap or Mediterranean veggies piled into a pita. Or go for an updated classic, like our South Beach Diet Club or Savory Egg Salad Sandwich. On Phase 1, you can enjoy many of our delicious sandwich fillings by simply removing the bread.

◀ *Chilled Roasted Red and Yellow Pepper Soup with Avocado Salsa (page 34)*

Chilled Roasted Red and Yellow Pepper Soup with Avocado Salsa

PREP TIME: 20 minutes   COOK TIME: 10 minutes   CHILL TIME: 30 minutes

This stunning soup is surprisingly quick and simple to make. Using roasted red and yellow peppers from a jar is convenient, but when you have a little more time, try roasting your own for a deeper, smoky flavor.

Soup

- 1 tablespoon extra-virgin olive oil
- 1 large onion, chopped
- ¼ teaspoon salt
- 2 cups lower-sodium chicken broth
- 2 roasted yellow peppers (from a jar), rinsed
- 2 roasted red peppers (from a jar), rinsed
- 1 cup low-fat or nonfat plain yogurt

Salsa

- ½ small avocado, finely chopped
- 1 tablespoon chopped fresh cilantro
- 1½ teaspoons fresh lime juice

For the soup: In a medium nonstick skillet, heat oil over medium heat; add onion and salt. Cook, stirring occasionally, until onion is softened, about 5 minutes. Add broth, bring to a boil, and simmer for 3 minutes; transfer to a medium bowl to cool.

Place half of the cooled broth mixture in a blender (make sure to get an equal amount of liquid and onions); add yellow peppers and ½ cup of the yogurt; purée until smooth. Transfer yellow pepper purée to a covered container and refrigerate until chilled, about 30 minutes. Rinse blender and transfer remaining broth mixture to it. Add red peppers and remaining ½ cup yogurt; purée until smooth. Transfer red pepper purée to another covered container and refrigerate until chilled, about 30 minutes.

For the salsa: While soups are chilling, in a small bowl combine avocado, cilantro, and lime juice.

To serve the soup, simultaneously ladle a generous ½ cup of the yellow pepper soup and a generous ½ cup of the red pepper soup into each of 4 shallow bowls, allowing soups to meet in center. Garnish each with salsa and serve.

Makes 4 (1-cup) servings

NUTRITION AT A GLANCE
Per serving: 160 calories, 9 g fat, 1.5 g saturated fat, 7 g protein, 12 g carbohydrate, 2 g fiber, 290 mg sodium

Indian Spiced Chilled Tomato Soup

PREP TIME: 10 minutes **COOK TIME:** 20 minutes **CHILL TIME:** 30 minutes

Wonderfully aromatic, cardamom adds a distinct and delicious Indian flavor to this tasty soup, which is also good served warm in cooler months.

- 1 tablespoon extra-virgin olive oil
- 1 teaspoon ground cardamom
- 1 teaspoon ground cumin
- ¼ teaspoon cayenne
- 1 onion, chopped
- 2 garlic cloves, minced
- ¼ teaspoon salt
- 1 (28-ounce) can whole peeled tomatoes, with juices
- 1⅓ cups low-fat or nonfat plain yogurt
- 1 tablespoon fresh lime juice

In a large nonstick skillet, heat oil over medium–high heat. Add cardamom, cumin, and cayenne; cook, stirring, until fragrant, about 30 seconds. Stir in onion, garlic, and salt; reduce the heat to medium and cook until onion is softened, about 5 minutes.

Add tomatoes and their juices, bring to a simmer, and cook for 10 minutes. Remove from the heat. Cool briefly and then stir in yogurt and lime juice.

Transfer half of the tomato mixture to a blender and purée until smooth; pour into a large bowl. Repeat with remaining tomato mixture; pour into the bowl. Cover and refrigerate until chilled, about 30 minutes. Serve chilled.

Makes 4 (1½-cup) servings

NUTRITION AT A GLANCE
Per serving: 150 calories, 5 g fat, 1.5 g saturated fat, 6 g protein, 17 g carbohydrate, 2 g fiber, 600 mg sodium

Curried Summer Squash Soup

PREP TIME: 15 minutes   **COOK TIME:** 15 minutes   **CHILL TIME:** 45 minutes

This flavorful soup gets its smooth texture from yogurt and puréed chickpeas, which also offer a nice hit of protein. It's satisfying chilled or warm.

- 1 tablespoon extra-virgin olive oil
- 2 teaspoons curry powder
- 2 medium yellow squash, chopped (3 cups)
- 1 large onion, coarsely chopped
- 3 cups lower-sodium chicken broth
- 1 (15.5-ounce) can chickpeas, rinsed and drained
  Salt and freshly ground black pepper
- ½ cup low-fat or nonfat plain yogurt
- 2 tablespoons chopped fresh basil

In a large saucepan, heat oil over medium-high heat. Add curry powder and cook, stirring, until fragrant, about 30 seconds. Stir in squash and onion, cover, and reduce the heat to medium. Cook, stirring occasionally, until squash is softened, about 8 minutes.

Add broth and chickpeas, bring to a simmer, and remove from the heat.

Transfer 2 cups of the soup to a blender and purée until smooth. Return puréed soup to the pan with the rest of the soup and stir to combine. Season with salt and pepper to taste.

Transfer soup to a covered container and refrigerate until chilled, about 45 minutes.

Divide soup among 4 bowls, top with a dollop of yogurt and a sprinkling of basil, and serve.

Makes 4 (1½-cup) servings

NUTRITION AT A GLANCE
Per serving: 200 calories, 5 g fat, 0.5 g saturated fat, 10 g protein, 30 g carbohydrate, 6 g fiber, 690 mg sodium

Summery Melon Soup

PREP TIME: 20 minutes   **CHILL TIME:** 30 minutes

Lemon juice, scallions, cucumber, and yogurt complement and mellow the sweetness of the honeydew in this refreshing soup. You can make it with cantaloupe, if you like.

- ½ (5-pound) honeydew, peeled and chopped (5 cups)
- 1 large cucumber, peeled and chopped
- ½ cup low-fat or nonfat plain yogurt
- 2 scallions, roughly chopped
- 1 tablespoon fresh lemon juice
- 2 teaspoons finely grated lemon zest

In a blender, purée honeydew until smooth. Add cucumber, yogurt, scallions, lemon juice, and 1 teaspoon of the zest; purée until smooth. Transfer soup to a covered container and refrigerate until chilled, about 30 minutes.

Divide soup among 4 bowls and sprinkle with remaining 1 teaspoon zest.

Makes 4 (1-cup) servings

NUTRITION AT A GLANCE
Per serving: 110 calories, 1 g fat, 0 g saturated fat, 3 g protein, 24 g carbohydrate, 2 g fiber, 60 mg sodium

Sweet Potato Vichyssoise

PREP TIME: 15 minutes   **COOK TIME:** 20 minutes   **CHILL TIME:** 45 minutes

Sweet potatoes provide a delicious twist on this classic chilled French soup and also offer an exceptional array of nutritional benefits, including a generous dose of vitamin B_6, vitamin C, iron, fiber, and beta-carotene.

- 2 medium sweet potatoes (1½ pounds), peeled and cut into 1-inch chunks
- 1 tablespoon extra-virgin olive oil
- 2 medium leeks, roots and tops trimmed and discarded, whites chopped (3 cups)
- 1 cup lower-sodium chicken broth
- 2 cups fat-free milk
- ¼ teaspoon salt
- 1 tablespoon chopped chives

Place sweet potatoes in a medium saucepan and add water to cover. Bring to a low boil and cook until sweet potatoes have softened, about 15 minutes. Drain in a colander and let cool briefly.

While sweet potatoes are cooking, in a medium nonstick skillet heat oil over medium heat. Add leeks, cover, and cook until softened, about 5 minutes. Add broth, bring to a simmer, and cook for 3 minutes more. Remove from the heat and let cool briefly.

In a blender, combine sweet potatoes, leeks, and broth; purée for 1 minute. Add milk and salt; purée until smooth. Transfer soup to a covered container and refrigerate until chilled, about 45 minutes.

Divide soup among 4 bowls, sprinkle with chives, and serve.

Makes 4 (1½-cup) servings

NUTRITION AT A GLANCE
Per serving: 160 calories, 4 g fat, 0.5 g saturated fat, 7 g protein, 24 g carbohydrate, 3 g fiber, 360 mg sodium

Cucumber Soup with Grilled Shrimp and Dill

PREP TIME: 20 minutes   **COOK TIME:** 5 minutes

Smoky grilled shrimp provide the perfect flavor and color balance for this lovely soup, which makes a light lunch or first course for an outdoor dinner. Try basil or mint in place of dill, if you like. Use a grill topper or basket to keep the shrimp from falling through the grate.

2 large cucumbers, peeled and roughly chopped

¾ cup cold water

1 cup low-fat or nonfat plain yogurt

1 tablespoon fresh lime juice

¼ teaspoon salt

¼ teaspoon freshly ground black pepper

¾ pound large shrimp, peeled and deveined

¼ cup chopped fresh dill

In a blender, combine cucumbers and water; purée for 30 seconds. Add yogurt, lime juice, salt, and pepper; purée until smooth.

Lightly coat a grill or grill pan with cooking spray and heat to medium-high. Grill shrimp just until pink, about 1 minute per side.

Divide soup among 4 bowls, top with shrimp and dill, and serve.

Makes 4 (1-cup) servings

NUTRITION AT A GLANCE
Per serving: 140 calories, 2.5 g fat, 1 g saturated fat, 19 g protein, 9 g carbohydrate, 1 g fiber, 300 mg sodium

Heirloom Tomato Gazpacho

PREP TIME: 30 minutes   **CHILL TIME:** 30 minutes

Remarkably flavorful heirloom tomatoes, which are grown from old-fashioned seed varieties, come in all shapes, sizes, and colors. Most are sweeter and juicier than conventional tomatoes. Here they turn gazpacho into something really special. Use any type of heirloom available at your local farmers' market. The color of your soup will vary accordingly.

2   pounds heirloom tomatoes, roughly chopped, plus 1 contrasting-color heirloom tomato for garnish

1   garlic clove, roughly chopped

1   large cucumber, peeled and roughly chopped

1   medium green bell pepper, roughly chopped

⅓   cup parsley leaves

½   small red onion, roughly chopped

1   small jalapeño, seeded and roughly chopped

1   cup ice cubes

1   tablespoon extra-virgin olive oil

1   tablespoon red wine vinegar

¼   teaspoon salt

In a blender, combine 2 pounds tomatoes and garlic; purée until smooth. Transfer to a large bowl.

In the blender, combine cucumber, bell pepper, parsley, onion, jalapeño, and ice; purée to a slightly chunky texture. Add to the bowl with tomato mixture. Stir in oil, vinegar, and salt. Transfer gazpacho to a covered container and refrigerate until chilled, about 30 minutes.

Just before serving, cut remaining tomato into small dice. Divide gazpacho among 4 shallow bowls, top with diced tomato, and serve.

Makes 4 (1½-cup) servings

NUTRITION AT A GLANCE
Per serving: 100 calories, 4.5 g fat, 0.5 g saturated fat, 3 g protein, 16 g carbohydrate, 4 g fiber, 170 mg sodium

White Gazpacho

PREP TIME: 20 minutes   **CHILL TIME: 30 minutes**

Made with almonds and bread, this rich, garlicky soup is a favorite in Spain, where almonds are an important nut crop. Serve it as a first course before Grilled Fish Tacos with Spicy Melon Salsa (page 102).

1   slice whole-grain bread, crust removed

1½ cups vegetable broth

½   cup slivered almonds

1   large cucumber, peeled and chopped

1   medium yellow bell pepper, chopped

4   scallions, chopped

1   tablespoon red wine vinegar

6   seedless green grapes, halved

Place bread in a blender and cover with broth; let sit until bread begins to soften, about 3 minutes.

Reserve 2 tablespoons of the almonds; add remaining 6 tablespoons almonds to the blender and purée until very smooth, about 1 minute. Add cucumber, pepper, scallions, and vinegar to the blender; purée until mixture is slightly chunky.

Transfer soup to a covered container and refrigerate until chilled, about 30 minutes. To serve, divide soup among 4 bowls and top with reserved almonds and grape halves.

Makes 4 (1-cup) servings

NUTRITION AT A GLANCE
Per serving: 150 calories, 9 g fat, 0.5 g saturated fat, 6 g protein, 14 g carbohydrate, 4 g fiber, 210 mg sodium

Garden White Bean Soup

PREP TIME: 25 minutes   COOK TIME: 25 minutes

Speckled with arugula and fresh basil, this smooth soup can be made with vegetable broth for an all-veggie version. Parmesan cheese sprinkled on top pulls all of the flavors together.

- 1 tablespoon plus 2 teaspoons extra-virgin olive oil
- 1 medium onion, thinly sliced
- 4 garlic cloves, thinly sliced
- 1 celery stalk, thinly sliced
- Pinch red pepper flakes
- 2 (15-ounce) cans Great Northern or cannellini beans, rinsed and drained
- 3 cups lower-sodium chicken broth
- 1½ cups packed chopped arugula
- ¼ cup packed basil leaves, roughly chopped
- ¼ teaspoon grated lemon zest
- ¼ teaspoon salt
- 4 tablespoons freshly grated Parmesan cheese

In a medium saucepan, heat 1 tablespoon of the oil over medium heat. Add onion, garlic, celery, and pepper flakes. Reduce the heat to medium-low and cook, stirring occasionally, until vegetables are softened, 10 to 12 minutes. Add beans and broth, bring to a simmer, and cook for 10 minutes. Remove from the heat and carefully strain liquid into a large bowl.

Transfer bean mixture to a blender or food processor, add 1 cup of the reserved liquid, remaining 2 teaspoons oil, arugula, basil, lemon zest, and salt; purée until smooth. Add to the bowl with the rest of the reserved cooking liquid and stir to combine.

Ladle soup into 4 bowls, sprinkle evenly with cheese, and serve warm.

Makes 4 (1¼-cup) servings

NUTRITION AT A GLANCE
Per serving: 290 calories, 8 g fat, 2 g saturated fat, 17 g protein, 40 g carbohydrate, 9 g fiber, 660 mg sodium

Savory Egg Salad Sandwiches

PREP TIME: 15 minutes   **COOK TIME:** 10 minutes   **STAND TIME:** 20 minutes

Our creamy egg salad is lighter than most because we use more whites than yolks. Refrigerate the leftover yolks in a covered container for up to 3 days. They're delicious chopped and sprinkled over salads, adding protein and vitamins A and D.

8 large eggs

½ small red onion, minced

2 celery stalks, minced

4 large green olives, chopped (optional)

3 tablespoons mayonnaise

1 teaspoon Dijon mustard

¼ teaspoon salt

4 slices whole-grain bread, toasted (optional)

1½ cups baby arugula

Place eggs in a medium saucepan, cover with water, and bring to a boil. Remove from the heat, cover, and let eggs sit for 20 minutes. Drain and place eggs in a bowl filled with ice water. When cool enough to handle, peel eggs.

In a medium bowl, mash 5 whole eggs and 3 egg whites together with the back of a fork. Add onion, celery, olives, if using, mayonnaise, mustard, and salt; stir to combine. Cover bread slices, if using, evenly with arugula, top with egg salad, and serve open face.

Makes 4 servings

NUTRITION AT A GLANCE

Per serving with bread: 270 calories, 16 g fat, 3 g saturated fat, 15 g protein, 16 g carbohydrate, 5 g fiber, 500 mg sodium

Per serving without bread: 190 calories, 15 g fat, 3 g saturated fat, 11 g protein, 2 g carbohydrate, 1 g fiber, 370 mg sodium

Pan Bagnat

PREP TIME: 30 minutes COOK TIME: 15 minutes MARINATING TIME: 30 minutes

A great take-along to the beach or a picnic, pan bagnat means "soaked bread," which also lends a clue to what makes this traditional French sandwich so delicious. After it is assembled, the sandwich is tightly wrapped and then compressed with a heavy skillet. Traditionally, it is refrigerated (while being pressed) overnight so that the juices seep into the bread. Try making this a day ahead, if you can wait!

- 4 ounces green beans, trimmed and cut into 1-inch pieces
- 1 tablespoon extra-virgin olive oil
- 1 teaspoon Dijon mustard
- 1 teaspoon red wine vinegar
- 1 (12-ounce) loaf whole-wheat peasant bread
- 2 (6-ounce) cans water-packed chunk light tuna, drained and flaked
- 2 medium plum tomatoes, sliced
- 2 hard-boiled eggs, sliced
- 8 kalamata olives, pitted and sliced

Bring a medium saucepan of salted water to a boil. Add beans, return to a boil, and cook until crisp-tender, about 2 minutes. Drain in a colander and rinse under very cold water to stop cooking. Drain again and pat dry.

In a small bowl, whisk together oil, mustard, and vinegar.

Slice bread in half horizontally and then tear out the inner bread from both halves, leaving a ½-inch shell of bread in each half (use the torn-out bread for making bread crumbs). Layer tuna, tomatoes, eggs, green beans, and olives in the bottom half of the bread; drizzle with oil mixture. Place top on sandwich and wrap tightly with plastic wrap.

Compress sandwich by placing a heavy skillet on top of it. Let it sit, weighted down, for 30 minutes at room temperature. Remove from plastic wrap, cut into 4 wedges, and serve.

Makes 4 servings

NUTRITION AT A GLANCE
Per serving: 410 calories, 12 g fat, 1.5 g saturated fat, 31 g protein, 40 g carbohydrate, 4 g fiber, 880 mg sodium

Grilled Salmon Salad Sandwiches

PREP TIME: 15 minutes   **COOK TIME:** 12 minutes

Watercress and cucumber are classic partners—and a refined choice—for the creamy, delicate sour cream dressing in this summery sandwich, which could also be served in a whole-wheat pita. Or spoon the salad into lettuce leaf cups and skip the bread for a satisfying Phase 1 lunch.

1	pound skinless salmon fillet, about 1 inch thick
1½	cups watercress leaves, chopped
1	medium cucumber, peeled and chopped
2	tablespoons reduced-fat sour cream
1	tablespoon fresh lemon juice
1	tablespoon chopped fresh dill
8	slices thin-sliced whole-wheat bread (optional)

Lightly coat a grill or grill pan with cooking spray and heat to medium–high. Grill salmon until opaque in the center, 4 to 5 minutes per side. Transfer to a plate to cool.

In a large bowl, combine watercress, cucumber, sour cream, lemon juice, and dill. Using a fork, flake cooled salmon into the bowl; toss well.

Divide salad among 4 bread slices, if using, and cover with remaining bread. Cut in half and serve.

Makes 4 servings

NUTRITION AT A GLANCE
Per serving with bread: 310 calories, 14 g fat, 3 g saturated fat, 28 g protein, 19 g carbohydrate, 5 g fiber, 250 mg sodium

Per serving without bread: 230 calories, 13 g fat, 3 g saturated fat, 23 g protein, 2 g carbohydrate, 0 g fiber, 95 mg sodium

South Beach Diet Club Sandwiches

PREP TIME: 15 minutes   **COOK TIME:** 5 minutes

Club sandwiches are a poolside favorite in South Beach. Here we make what's known in restaurant lingo as a "junior" club because it features two slices of bread instead of the classic three. We've also updated ours with a spicy cumin mayonnaise.

- 2 tablespoons mayonnaise
- 1 tablespoon fresh lemon juice
- ½ teaspoon ground cumin
- ¼ teaspoon cayenne
- 4 slices Canadian bacon (about 1 ounce each)
- 8 slices thin-sliced whole-grain bread, lightly toasted
- 4 small red leaf lettuce leaves
- ¼ pound thinly sliced salt-free or reduced-sodium deli turkey breast
- ½ small avocado, cut into 4 slices
- 1 large beefsteak tomato, cut into 4 slices

In a small bowl, combine mayonnaise, lemon juice, cumin, and cayenne.

Lightly coat a large nonstick skillet with cooking spray and heat over medium–high heat. Add bacon and cook until edges begin to brown, about 1 minute per side. Transfer to a paper towel–lined plate.

Spread mayonnaise mixture on 4 toast slices. Top each with 1 lettuce leaf, one-fourth of the turkey, 1 avocado slice, 1 bacon slice, and 1 tomato slice; cover with remaining toast. Cut in half, secure with toothpicks, if necessary, and serve.

Makes 4 servings

NUTRITION AT A GLANCE
Per serving: 250 calories, 12 g fat, 2 g saturated fat, 19 g protein, 22 g carbohydrate, 7 g fiber, 630 mg sodium

Mediterranean Vegetable Sandwiches

PREP TIME: 30 minutes

The bright colors and flavors of this overstuffed sandwich reflect the sunny region it's named for. Soaking the onions in ice water tames the bite; try this technique for salads, too. If you're on Phase 1, skip the pita and eat the filling as a salad.

½ small red onion, very thinly sliced

1 (15.5-ounce) can chickpeas, rinsed and drained

1½ cups baby spinach

3 ounces reduced-fat feta cheese, crumbled (generous ⅓ cup)

1 medium cucumber, halved crosswise and thinly sliced lengthwise

1 large tomato, thinly sliced

2 roasted red peppers (from a jar), rinsed and cut into ¼-inch slices

¼ cup pitted kalamata olives, roughly chopped

1 tablespoon extra-virgin olive oil

1½ teaspoons red wine vinegar

⅛ teaspoon ground cumin

Cayenne

2 (6-inch) whole-grain pita breads, halved

Place onion in a small bowl and cover with ice water; let sit for 10 minutes.

Drain onion, pat dry, and place in a medium bowl. Add chickpeas, spinach, feta, cucumber, tomato, peppers, olives, oil, vinegar, and cumin; stir gently to combine. Season with cayenne to taste.

Fill pita halves with vegetable mixture and serve.

Makes 4 (½-pita) servings

NUTRITION AT A GLANCE

Per serving with pita: 290 calories, 9 g fat, 2.5 g saturated fat, 13 g protein, 44 g carbohydrate, 8 g fiber, 770 mg sodium

Per serving without pita: 204 calories, 8 g fat, 2 g saturated fat, 10 g protein, 26 g carbohydrate, 6 g fiber, 600 mg sodium

Classic Lobster Rolls

PREP TIME: 15 minutes   **COOK TIME:** 15 minutes

A perfect celebration of summer, this sandwich is elegant enough for dinner, served with Baby Greens with Tiny Tomatoes, Fresh Herbs, and Toasted Pistachios (page 74). Frozen lobster tails are convenient, but you can also purchase 1½ pounds of fresh lobster meat for four sandwiches.

4	frozen lobster tails, defrosted (about 1½ pounds)
1	small celery stalk, finely chopped
1	tablespoon minced red onion
1	tablespoon mayonnaise
1	tablespoon chopped tarragon leaves
1	teaspoon fresh lemon juice
¼	teaspoon salt
	Freshly ground black pepper
4	whole-wheat hot dog rolls, lightly toasted (optional)

Fill a large saucepan with enough water to come ½ inch up the side of the pan; cover and bring to a simmer. Add lobster tails, return to a simmer, and partially cover. Cook until lobster is opaque throughout, about 8 minutes. Remove lobster from the pan and let cool. When cool enough to handle, remove shells and chop lobster meat into bite-size pieces.

In a medium bowl, combine lobster, celery, onion, mayonnaise, tarragon, lemon juice, and salt. Season with pepper to taste. Divide lobster salad among 4 rolls, if using, and serve.

Makes 4 servings

NUTRITION AT A GLANCE
Per serving with roll: 300 calories, 6 g fat, 1 g saturated fat, 36 g protein, 23 g carbohydrate, 3 g fiber, 880 mg sodium
Per serving without roll: 180 calories, 4.5 g fat, 0.5 g saturated fat, 32 g protein, 1 g carbohydrate, 0 g fiber, 670 mg sodium

Monkfish and Shrimp Rolls

PREP TIME: 25 minutes   COOK TIME: 15 minutes

This combo sandwich makes a terrific salad: Increase the spinach, lightly dress it with a little olive oil and some fresh lemon juice, then spoon the citrusy fish on top. The addition of the orange keeps this recipe Phase 2, even without the roll.

1 seedless orange	1 tablespoon mayonnaise
1 lemon	¼ teaspoon salt
1 lime	12 small spinach leaves, thinly sliced
1 (8-ounce) monkfish fillet	
½ pound large shrimp, peeled and deveined	4 whole-wheat hot dog rolls, lightly toasted (optional)
½ small avocado, chopped	

Finely grate zest from orange, lemon, and lime over a small bowl; stir to combine. Place 1 teaspoon of the mixed zest in a medium bowl and place remaining zest in a medium skillet. Remove skin and white membrane from orange and chop the fruit. Add chopped orange to the bowl with zest.

Halve the lemon and lime and squeeze juice from both halves into the skillet. Add enough water to come ½ inch up the side of the pan, cover, and bring to a simmer. Add monkfish, return to a simmer, and cook, partially covered, until opaque in the center, about 5 minutes per side. Using a slotted spoon, transfer fish to a cutting board and cut into small chunks.

Bring liquid in the skillet back to a simmer, add shrimp, and simmer until shrimp turn pink, 1 to 2 minutes. Transfer shrimp to the cutting board and slice lengthwise. Add shrimp and monkfish to the bowl with orange mixture. Add avocado, mayonnaise, and salt; toss gently to combine.

Divide spinach leaves among rolls, if using, spoon salad evenly on top, and serve.

Makes 4 servings

NUTRITION AT A GLANCE
Per serving with roll: 300 calories, 10 g fat, 1.5 g saturated fat, 24 g protein, 32 g carbohydrate, 6 g fiber, 480 mg sodium
Per serving without roll: 190 calories, 8 g fat, 1 g saturated fat, 20 g protein, 10 g carbohydrate, 3 g fiber, 280 mg sodium

Cool Cod Sandwiches with Homemade Tartar Sauce

PREP TIME: 10 minutes   COOK TIME: 10 minutes

Creamy tartar sauce is a warm-weather favorite, especially when spiked with tangy cornichon pickles and capers. It's delicious here atop skillet-cooked cod. If you're on Phase 1, simply skip the bun.

Sauce

- 2 tablespoons mayonnaise
- 2 tablespoons chopped cornichons
- 2 teaspoons capers, rinsed, drained, and chopped
- 1 tablespoon fresh lemon juice

Sandwich

- 4 (6-ounce) cod fillets, about 1 inch thick
- ⅛ teaspoon salt
- 1 tablespoon extra-virgin olive oil
- 2 romaine lettuce leaves, torn in half
- 4 whole-grain sandwich buns, lightly toasted (optional)

For the sauce: In a small bowl, combine mayonnaise, cornichons, capers, and lemon juice.

For the sandwich: Sprinkle cod with salt. In a large nonstick skillet, heat oil over medium–high heat. Add cod and cook until golden on the outside and opaque inside, 4 to 5 minutes per side. Place lettuce and cod on buns, if using, dollop each with 1 tablespoon tartar sauce, and serve.

Makes 4 servings

NUTRITION AT A GLANCE
Per serving with bun: 380 calories, 13 g fat, 2 g saturated fat, 37 g protein, 27 g carbohydrate, 3 g fiber, 650 mg sodium
Per serving without bun: 230 calories, 10 g fat, 1.5 g saturated fat, 31 g protein, 3 g carbohydrate, 0 g fiber, 420 mg sodium

Chipotle-Rubbed Steak Wraps

PREP TIME: 20 minutes   **MARINATING TIME:** 1 hour   **COOK TIME:** 20 minutes   **STAND TIME:** 5 minutes

Chipotle chiles in adobo (a sauce made from puréed chiles, vinegar, and spices) flavor the steak in this spicy wrap. Look for them canned in the Latin American section of larger supermarkets. Leftover chiles can be used to season beans, burritos, soups, and more. Store them in a sealed container in the refrigerator or freezer.

1	tablespoon chopped chipotle chiles in adobo, or more to taste
1	(1¼-pound) flank steak, about 1 inch thick
2	large romaine lettuce leaves, shredded
2	medium plum tomatoes, chopped
1	tablespoon reduced-fat sour cream
2	teaspoons fresh lime juice
¼	teaspoon salt
4	(8-inch) whole-wheat wraps

Rub chiles onto both sides of steak; place steak in a resealable plastic bag and let marinate at room temperature for 1 hour.

Heat the broiler and broiler pan for 10 minutes. Place steak on broiler pan and cook for 4 to 5 minutes per side for medium-rare. Remove from the broiler, transfer to a cutting board, and let steak rest for 5 minutes. Cut into thin slices across the grain.

In a medium bowl, combine lettuce, tomatoes, sour cream, lime juice, and salt.

Heat wraps in the oven or microwave according to package directions. Divide lettuce mixture and steak evenly among wraps, roll up, and serve.

Makes 4 servings

NUTRITION AT A GLANCE
Per serving: 360 calories, 15 g fat, 5 g saturated fat, 36 g protein, 27 g carbohydrate, 8 g fiber, 580 mg sodium

SUNSATIONAL SALADS AND SIDES

Local farmers' markets and gardens are filled to the brim with a dizzying array of fresh fruits, vegetables, and herbs all summer long. With treasures like these, it's easy to make the tasty salads and side dishes in the coming pages.

Start a great meal with Green and Yellow Beans with Fresh Mozzarella and Pine Nuts or Crisp Jícama Salad with Creamy Cilantro Dressing. Or serve a hearty, protein-rich dish—like Grilled Southwest Steak, Radish, and Blue Cheese Salad—as a satisfying main course. When shopping, look for fresh herbs, ripe tomatoes, shiny eggplants, and firm cucumbers.

Our side dishes, including Spicy Grilled Sweet Potato Fries, Grilled Eggplant Rounds with Garlicky Cilantro Topping, Picnic Macaroni Salad, and Southern-Style Greens, are especially geared for easygoing dining, indoors or out. For a fun summer party, prepare several salads and sides, grill your choice of chicken, meat, or fish, and enjoy!

◄ *Green and Yellow Beans with Fresh Mozzarella and Pine Nuts (page 62)*

Green and Yellow Beans with Fresh Mozzarella and Pine Nuts

PREP TIME: 10 minutes   **COOK TIME:** 10 minutes

Lovers of the Italian mozzarella, tomato, and basil salad known as Caprese will enjoy this colorful twist, made with two kinds of beans. In place of the string beans, you can try broad, flat Italian green beans, which are also called Romano beans. Toasted pine nuts add protein and delicious flavor.

- 2 tablespoons pine nuts
- 8 ounces green beans, trimmed
- 8 ounces yellow wax beans, trimmed
- 1 tablespoon extra-virgin olive oil
- ¼ teaspoon salt
- ⅛ teaspoon freshly ground black pepper
- 4 ounces fresh part-skim mozzarella cheese
- ¼ cup basil leaves, sliced

Heat the oven to 275°F. Spread pine nuts on a baking sheet and toast until fragrant and lightly golden, 5 to 7 minutes. Set aside.

While pine nuts are toasting, bring a large saucepan of water to a boil. Add beans and cook just until crisp-tender, about 3 minutes. Drain in a colander and run under very cold water for 1 minute to stop cooking. Drain again and pat dry. Transfer beans to a medium bowl and toss with oil, salt, and pepper.

Slice cheese into 4 thin slices and cut each slice in half so that you have 8 half-circles. Divide cheese slices and beans among 4 salad plates, alternating the green and yellow beans with the cheese slices. Sprinkle with basil and pine nuts and serve.

Makes 4 servings

NUTRITION AT A GLANCE
Per serving: 180 calories, 13 g fat, 5 g saturated fat, 8 g protein, 9 g carbohydrate, 4 g fiber, 190 mg sodium

Seafood Caesar

PREP TIME: 20 minutes   **COOK TIME:** 8 minutes

Everybody loves a crisp, creamy Caesar salad, and when you add our garlic-and-lemon-grilled shrimp along with fresh lump crabmeat, it gets even better! If you're grilling outdoors, skewer the shrimp or use a grill topper to keep the shrimp from falling through the grate.

¾ pound large shrimp (about 16), peeled and deveined

2 teaspoons plus 2 tablespoons extra-virgin olive oil

2 garlic cloves, minced

1 teaspoon grated lemon zest

¼ teaspoon freshly ground black pepper

2 teaspoons fresh lemon juice

4 anchovy fillets, minced, or 2 teaspoons anchovy paste

1 teaspoon Dijon mustard

1 (1-pound) head romaine lettuce, chopped (8 cups)

1 tablespoon freshly grated Parmesan cheese

½ pound lump crabmeat (about 1 cup)

In a medium bowl, toss shrimp with 2 teaspoons of the oil, half of the garlic, lemon zest, and pepper.

Lightly coat a grill or grill pan with cooking spray and heat to medium-high. Grill shrimp until they turn pink, 2 to 3 minutes per side. Remove from the heat and set aside.

In a large bowl, whisk together lemon juice, anchovies, mustard, and remaining garlic. Slowly whisk in remaining 2 tablespoons oil. Add lettuce and cheese and toss well. Divide lettuce among 4 plates, top with shrimp and crab, and serve.

Makes 4 (2-cup) servings

NUTRITION AT A GLANCE
Per serving: 207 calories, 12 g fat, 2 g saturated fat, 20 g protein, 5 g carbohydrate, 2 g fiber, 391 mg sodium

Poached Chicken, Zucchini, and Wheat Berry Salad

PREP TIME: 10 minutes   STAND TIME: 20 minutes   COOK TIME: 50 minutes

Wheat berries add delicious nutty flavor—as well as protein, fiber, and B vitamins—to this tasty salad. The soft variety of wheat berries used here cooks faster than hard wheat berries and doesn't need to be soaked for long.

½ cup soft wheat berries	1 medium zucchini, peeled into thin strips
1¾ cups lower-sodium chicken broth	½ cup nonfat plain yogurt
1 pound boneless, skinless chicken breasts	1 tablespoon extra-virgin olive oil
Freshly ground black pepper	⅛ teaspoon salt
1½ cups water	4 large Boston lettuce leaves
3 teaspoons fresh lemon juice	¼ cup basil leaves, thinly sliced

Place wheat berries in a medium saucepan and cover with about 2 inches of water. Bring to a boil over medium-high heat, turn off the heat, and cover. Let stand for 15 to 20 minutes.

Drain and return wheat berries to the pan. Add broth and bring to a boil over medium-high heat. Reduce the heat, cover, and simmer until the broth is absorbed and the berries are firm but not crunchy, 40 to 45 minutes. Transfer wheat berries to a large bowl.

While wheat berries are cooking, lightly season chicken with pepper. In a large nonstick skillet, combine chicken, water, and 1 teaspoon of the lemon juice; bring to a simmer over medium heat. Reduce the heat to low, cover, and simmer until chicken is cooked through, 10 to 15 minutes, turning once halfway through cooking. Remove chicken from liquid, transfer to a cutting board, and when cool enough to handle, cut into ½-inch cubes.

Add chicken and zucchini to the bowl with cooked wheat berries.

In a small bowl, whisk together yogurt, oil, salt, and remaining 2 teaspoons lemon juice. Pour dressing over chicken mixture and toss to combine. Divide lettuce leaves among 4 salad plates. Spoon chicken mixture onto lettuce, sprinkle with basil, and serve.

Makes 4 (1-cup) servings

NUTRITION AT A GLANCE
Per serving: 260 calories, 5 g fat, 1 g saturated fat, 33 g protein, 22 g carbohydrate, 4 g fiber, 460 mg sodium

Summer's Bounty Greek Salad

PREP TIME: 15 minutes   **COOK TIME:** 15 minutes

Bursting with juicy tomatoes, snappy green beans, and cooling cukes, this salad is an easy put-together for any night of the week. If you have additional fresh herbs around, toss them in, too. Chopped chives and whole basil leaves are particularly nice.

- 8 ounces green beans, trimmed
- 1 (12-ounce) head romaine lettuce, chopped (6 cups)
- 2 medium tomatoes, cut into wedges
- 1 medium cucumber, halved lengthwise, seeded, and thinly sliced
- 4 ounces reduced-fat feta cheese, crumbled (⅔ cup)
- ¼ cup pitted kalamata olives, sliced
- 2 tablespoons extra-virgin olive oil
- 1 tablespoon red wine vinegar
- ⅛ teaspoon salt
- ⅛ teaspoon freshly ground black pepper
- ¼ cup chopped fresh parsley

Bring a large saucepan of lightly salted water to a boil. Add beans and cook just until crisp-tender, about 3 minutes. Drain in a colander and run under very cold water for 1 minute to stop cooking. Drain again and pat dry. Cut beans into 1-inch pieces.

In a large bowl, combine beans, lettuce, tomatoes, cucumber, feta, and olives. In a small bowl, whisk together oil, vinegar, salt, and pepper; pour over salad and toss to coat. Divide salad among 4 plates and sprinkle with parsley just before serving.

Makes 4 (2½-cup) servings

NUTRITION AT A GLANCE
Per serving: 180 calories, 12 g fat, 3 g saturated fat, 9 g protein, 13 g carbohydrate, 6 g fiber, 550 mg sodium

Endive Salad with Walnuts

PREP TIME: 10 minutes   **COOK TIME:** 10 minutes

This crisp salad is refreshing before or after a main course and also works well as a side dish with grilled chicken or fish. Look for tight heads of Belgian endive free from brown spots.

- ½ cup walnut halves
- 1 tablespoon extra-virgin olive oil
- 1 teaspoon Dijon mustard
- 1 teaspoon red wine vinegar
- 4 heads Belgian endive (1 pound)
- ¼ teaspoon salt
- ⅛ teaspoon freshly ground black pepper

Heat the oven to 350°F. Spread walnuts on a baking sheet and toast until fragrant and lightly browned, about 10 minutes.

In a large bowl, whisk together oil, mustard, and vinegar. Trim endives, halve each head lengthwise, then cut lengthwise into long, thin strips. Add endive, walnuts, salt, and pepper to the bowl with dressing; toss to combine. Divide salad among 4 salad plates and serve.

Makes 4 (1-cup) servings

NUTRITION AT A GLANCE
Per serving: 130 calories, 12 g fat, 1.5 g saturated fat, 3 g protein, 6 g carbohydrate, 4 g fiber, 160 mg sodium

Honeydew, Fresh Herb, and Ricotta Salata Salad

PREP TIME: 10 minutes

When fresh ricotta goes through its natural aging process for at least 3 months, a smooth, firm cheese suitable for shaving or grating results. In this refreshing salad, the slight tang of this Italian sheep's milk cheese perks up the melon and fresh herbs. Use a vegetable peeler to shave it. Ricotta salata is available in the cheese section of larger supermarkets or at cheese shops. Reduced-fat feta is a good substitute.

1   (4- to 5-pound) honeydew melon, scooped into balls (4 cups)

1   cucumber, peeled and thinly sliced

1   tablespoon plus 1 teaspoon extra-virgin olive oil

1½ teaspoons red wine vinegar

¼   teaspoon salt

⅛   teaspoon freshly ground black pepper

¼   cup packed basil leaves, thinly sliced

2   tablespoons chopped fresh parsley

2   ounces ricotta salata cheese

In a large bowl, combine melon and cucumber. In a small bowl, whisk together oil, vinegar, salt, and pepper; pour over melon and cucumber and toss to coat. Add basil and parsley and toss to combine. Divide salad among 4 bowls, cups, or plates, shave cheese over the top, and serve.

Makes 4 (1½-cup) servings

NUTRITION AT A GLANCE
Per serving: 160 calories, 8 g fat, 3 g saturated fat, 4 g protein, 20 g carbohydrate, 2 g fiber, 420 mg sodium

Crisp Jícama Salad with Creamy Cilantro Dressing

PREP TIME: 15 minutes

Jícama is a delicious root vegetable that's most often enjoyed raw. It's perfect for salads and slaws because of its crisp texture and slightly sweet flavor. The papery yellow skin comes off easily with a vegetable peeler.

½ cup nonfat or low-fat plain yogurt

¼ cup finely chopped fresh cilantro

3 tablespoons fresh lime juice

2 tablespoons extra-virgin olive oil

¼ teaspoon salt

⅛ teaspoon freshly ground black pepper

1 (10-ounce) head red leaf lettuce, chopped (6 cups)

1 (1-pound) jícama, peeled and cut into matchsticks

1 medium cucumber, seeded and thinly sliced

In a small bowl, combine yogurt, cilantro, lime juice, oil, salt, and pepper. Place lettuce in a large bowl and toss with ¼ cup of the dressing; divide among 4 salad plates. Add jícama and cucumber to the same large bowl and toss with remaining dressing. Spoon jícama and cucumber mixture on top of lettuce and serve.

Makes 4 (2½-cup) servings

NUTRITION AT A GLANCE
Per serving: 130 calories, 7 g fat, 1 g saturated fat, 4 g protein, 13 g carbohydrate, 1 g fiber, 190 mg sodium

Romaine Hearts with Tuna, Edamame, and Green Goddess Dressing

PREP TIME: 10 minutes

This light salad makes a great summer lunch or a side salad for a larger meal (without the tuna). The creamy Green Goddess Dressing is our (anchovy-less) version of the original, which was created in the 1920s by the chef of San Francisco's Palace Hotel for George Arliss, who was starring in William Archer's hit play, The Green Goddess. *If you don't have all of the fresh herbs called for here, simply double up on the ones that you do have.*

½ medium avocado

3 tablespoons mayonnaise

3 tablespoons nonfat or low-fat plain yogurt

1 tablespoon water

2 scallions, chopped

1 small garlic clove

2 tablespoons chopped fresh basil

1 tablespoon chopped fresh parsley

1 tablespoon chopped fresh tarragon

2 teaspoons fresh lemon juice

¼ teaspoon salt

⅛ teaspoon freshly ground black pepper

3 romaine hearts, chopped (8 cups)

2 (6-ounce) cans water-packed chunk light tuna, drained and flaked

1 cup frozen shelled edamame, defrosted

In a blender, combine avocado, mayonnaise, yogurt, water, scallions, and garlic; purée until smooth. Add basil, parsley, tarragon, lemon juice, salt, and pepper; blend just until combined.

In a large bowl, combine romaine, tuna, and edamame. Add dressing and toss. Serve at room temperature.

Makes 4 (2-cup) servings

NUTRITION AT A GLANCE
Per serving: 280 calories, 15 g fat, 2.5 g saturated fat, 27 g protein, 9 g carbohydrate, 4 g fiber, 500 mg sodium

Grilled Southwest Steak, Radish, and Blue Cheese Salad

PREP TIME: 15 minutes   COOK TIME: 10 minutes

Chili powder and fresh garlic give the steak a robust flavor that complements the crisp romaine and spicy radishes in this hearty Tex-Mex salad.

- 2 garlic cloves, minced
- 1 tablespoon chili powder
- 2 teaspoons ground cumin
- ¼ teaspoon salt
- ¼ teaspoon freshly ground black pepper
- 1¼ pounds lean sirloin steak, about ¾ inch thick
- 1 (12-ounce) head romaine lettuce, chopped (6 cups)
- 8 large radishes, cut into wedges, plus whole radishes for garnish
- 4 ounces blue cheese, crumbled (½ cup)
- 1 tablespoon extra-virgin olive oil
- 1 tablespoon fresh lime juice

In a small bowl, combine garlic, chili powder, cumin, ⅛ teaspoon of the salt, and ⅛ teaspoon of the pepper. Rub spice mixture onto steak.

Lightly coat a grill or grill pan with cooking spray and heat to medium-high. Grill steak about 4 minutes per side for medium-rare. Transfer to a cutting board and let rest for 5 minutes before cutting into thin slices.

In a large bowl, combine lettuce, radishes, cheese, oil, lime juice, and remaining ⅛ teaspoon salt and ⅛ teaspoon pepper. Divide salad among 4 plates, top with steak slices, and garnish with whole radishes. Serve warm.

Makes 4 servings

NUTRITION AT A GLANCE
Per serving: 360 calories, 19 g fat, 8 g saturated fat, 39 g protein, 7 g carbohydrate, 3 g fiber, 680 mg sodium

Baby Greens with Tiny Tomatoes, Fresh Herbs, and Toasted Pistachios

PREP TIME: 15 minutes   **COOK TIME: 8 minutes**

This beautiful salad can be gussied up with baby heirloom tomatoes or an assortment of pear tomatoes, grape tomatoes, and currant tomatoes. Pistachios, sprinkled on top, are rich in potassium, phosphorus, and magnesium.

½ cup unsalted shelled pistachios

6 ounces mixed baby greens (6 cups)

1½ cups cherry tomatoes, halved

1 medium cucumber, thinly sliced

¼ cup basil leaves, roughly chopped

¼ cup mint leaves, roughly chopped

1 tablespoon extra-virgin olive oil

2 teaspoons sherry vinegar

¼ teaspoon salt

⅛ teaspoon freshly ground black pepper

Heat the oven to 350°F. Spread pistachios on a baking sheet; toast until golden brown, about 8 minutes. Transfer to a cutting board and roughly chop.

In a large bowl, combine greens, tomatoes, cucumber, basil, and mint. Add oil, vinegar, salt, and pepper; toss to coat. Divide salad among 4 plates, sprinkle with pistachios, and serve.

Makes 4 (2-cup) servings

NUTRITION AT A GLANCE
Per serving: 160 calories, 11 g fat, 1.5 g saturated fat, 6 g protein, 13 g carbohydrate, 5 g fiber, 180 mg sodium

Grilled Asparagus with Lemon Aioli

PREP TIME: 10 minutes   **COOK TIME: 10 minutes**

Asparagus is ideal for grilling because it holds its shape. Use medium-thick or thick spears and periodically turn them with a pair of long-handled tongs. Nutritionally, asparagus is low in fat and high in fiber and provides iron, B vitamins, and vitamin C.

- ¼ cup mayonnaise
- ½ teaspoon grated lemon zest
- 1 teaspoon fresh lemon juice
- 2 garlic cloves, minced
- ¼ teaspoon salt
- ⅛ teaspoon freshly ground black pepper
- 1½ pounds medium-thick asparagus, trimmed
- 2 teaspoons extra-virgin olive oil

Lightly coat a grill or grill pan with cooking spray and heat to medium-high.

In a small bowl, whisk together mayonnaise, lemon zest, lemon juice, garlic, ⅛ teaspoon of the salt, and pepper.

In a large bowl, toss asparagus with oil and remaining ⅛ teaspoon salt. Grill asparagus, turning occasionally, until lightly browned and tender, 8 to 10 minutes. Divide asparagus among 4 plates, spoon aioli on top, and serve.

Makes 4 servings

NUTRITION AT A GLANCE
Per serving: 150 calories, 14 g fat, 2 g saturated fat, 3 g protein, 6 g carbohydrate, 3 g fiber, 240 mg sodium

Moroccan Couscous

PREP TIME: 10 minutes   **COOK TIME:** 10 minutes

Redolent with aromatic spices, this easy side dish takes just minutes to prepare and can be served with any grilled or pan-cooked meat or fish or with a platter of assorted grilled or roasted vegetables. When good, ripe tomatoes aren't available, use ¾ cup of canned diced tomatoes instead.

- ½ cup whole-wheat couscous
- 1½ teaspoons ground cumin
- 1 teaspoon paprika
- ½ teaspoon ground cinnamon
- ¼ teaspoon salt
- ⅛ teaspoon freshly ground black pepper
- Pinch cayenne
- 1 tomato, chopped
- ⅓ cup minced red onion
- 1 tablespoon extra-virgin olive oil
- 2 teaspoons fresh lemon juice
- 3 tablespoons minced fresh parsley

Prepare couscous according to package directions.

In a small bowl, combine cumin, paprika, cinnamon, salt, pepper, and cayenne.

Fluff cooked couscous with a fork. Add cumin mixture, tomato, onion, oil, and lemon juice; stir to combine. Divide among 4 plates, sprinkle with parsley, and serve warm.

Makes 4 (½-cup) servings

NUTRITION AT A GLANCE
Per serving: 100 calories, 4 g fat, 0.5 g saturated fat, 3 g protein, 15 g carbohydrate, 3 g fiber, 150 mg sodium

Grilled Eggplant Rounds with Garlicky Cilantro Topping

PREP TIME: 10 minutes   **COOK TIME:** 10 minutes

Easy to grill, eggplant is flavored here with a chili powder rub and served with a sprinkle of fresh cilantro and garlic. Choose eggplants that are heavy for their size and have a nice, smooth skin. If you use white eggplants, peel them first; the skin is very tough.

1   tablespoon chili powder

1   teaspoon ground cumin

¼   teaspoon salt

2   tablespoons finely chopped fresh cilantro, plus sprigs for garnish

1   garlic clove, minced

2   medium eggplants (about 2 pounds), cut into 20 (½-inch-thick) rounds

Lightly coat a grill or grill pan with cooking spray and heat to medium–high.

In a small bowl, stir together chili powder, cumin, and salt. In another small bowl, stir together cilantro and garlic.

Using a sharp paring knife, score a crisscross pattern on both sides of eggplant rounds; season both sides of rounds with chili powder mixture.

Grill eggplant until softened, 4 to 5 minutes per side; transfer to a serving platter. Sprinkle eggplant with cilantro mixture, garnish with cilantro sprigs, and serve hot.

Makes 4 (5-piece) servings

NUTRITION AT A GLANCE

Per serving: 60 calories, 0.5 g fat, 0 g saturated fat, 2 g protein, 13 g carbohydrate, 8 g fiber, 151 mg sodium

Picnic Macaroni Salad

PREP TIME: 10 minutes   **COOK TIME:** 20 minutes

This creamy barbecue and picnic classic is a favorite of kids and adults alike. It stores well in a covered container in the refrigerator, and its flavors deepen over time, so try making it up to a day in advance. If you like pickles in your macaroni salad, use cornichons. They add just the right touch of pickle flavor without the sugar you find in the often-used pickle relish.

1½	cups whole-wheat or spelt elbow pasta
2	medium tomatoes, chopped
1	medium red bell pepper, diced
1	medium carrot, diced
⅓	cup reduced-fat sour cream
¼	cup chopped cornichons (optional)
2	tablespoons mayonnaise
1	teaspoon dried oregano
¼	teaspoon salt
⅛	teaspoon freshly ground black pepper

Bring a large pot of lightly salted water to a boil. Cook pasta according to package directions until al dente. Drain, run under cold water to cool, and drain again.

In a large bowl, combine pasta, tomatoes, bell pepper, carrot, sour cream, cornichons, if using, mayonnaise, oregano, salt, and black pepper. Serve at room temperature or chilled.

Makes 8 (generous ½-cup) servings

NUTRITION AT A GLANCE
Per serving: 120 calories, 4.5 g fat, 1 g saturated fat, 4 g protein, 18 g carbohydrate, 3 g fiber, 105 mg sodium

Summertime Sweet Potato Salad

PREP TIME: 10 minutes   **COOK TIME:** 20 minutes

Yogurt and red wine vinegar make a smooth and tasty dressing for this easy picnic dish. Tarragon can be added or used as a substitute for basil. Since sweet potatoes are available year-round, try serving this dish warm in cooler months; simply drain the potatoes and don't rinse them before adding the dressing.

  2   medium sweet potatoes (1½ pounds), peeled and cut into 1-inch cubes
  ⅓   cup nonfat or low-fat plain yogurt
  1   small red bell pepper, diced
  2   scallions, thinly sliced
  3   tablespoons chopped fresh basil
  1   teaspoon red wine vinegar
  ¼   teaspoon salt
  ⅛   teaspoon freshly ground black pepper

Place sweet potatoes in a medium saucepan and add cold water to cover. Bring to a boil and cook until tender, 8 to 10 minutes. Drain, run under cold water to cool, and drain again.

  In a large bowl, combine sweet potatoes, yogurt, bell pepper, scallions, basil, vinegar, salt, and black pepper. Serve at room temperature or chilled.

Makes 4 (generous ¾-cup) servings

NUTRITION AT A GLANCE
Per serving: 120 calories, 0 g fat, 0 g saturated fat, 4 g protein, 27 g carbohydrate, 4 g fiber, 210 mg sodium

Grilled Fennel with Mixed Olives

PREP TIME: 10 minutes   **COOK TIME:** 10 minutes

This tasty Mediterranean-style side is great with grilled chicken or meaty fish like tuna or sea bass. When the weather cools, you can make this dish on a grill pan indoors.

2	large fennel bulbs, trimmed and cut lengthwise into 2-inch wedges (do not core)
⅛	teaspoon salt
	Pinch freshly ground black pepper
½	cup pitted mixed olives, roughly chopped
1	tablespoon extra-virgin olive oil
2	teaspoons grated lemon zest
1½	teaspoons fresh lemon juice

Lightly coat a grill or grill pan with cooking spray and heat to medium-high.

Season fennel with salt and pepper. Grill until tender, 4 to 5 minutes per side. Transfer fennel to a cutting board and remove any tough core from wedges.

In a large bowl, toss fennel with olives, oil, lemon zest, and lemon juice. Serve warm or at room temperature.

Makes 4 (¾-cup) servings

NUTRITION AT A GLANCE
Per serving: 90 calories, 6 g fat, 0.5 g saturated fat, 2 g protein, 10 g carbohydrate, 4 g fiber, 290 mg sodium

Grilled Chipotle Onion Rings

PREP TIME: 10 minutes   **COOK TIME:** 12 minutes

Try red, yellow, or sweet onions (such as Vidalia)—or a mix of all three—to make these sweet and spicy onion rings. When cooking on an outdoor grill, use a grill topper or vegetable basket so the onions don't slip through the grate.

- 2 medium onions, cut into ½-inch-thick rounds
- ¼ teaspoon salt
- ⅛ teaspoon freshly ground black pepper
- 2 canned chipotle chiles in adobo, rinsed, seeded, and minced
- 2 teaspoons fresh lime juice

Lightly coat a grill or grill pan with cooking spray and heat to medium-high.

In a medium bowl, toss onions with salt and pepper (rings can separate). Grill onions, turning occasionally, until lightly browned, 10 to 12 minutes. Return onions to bowl, add chiles and lime juice, and toss until the onions are well coated. Serve warm.

Makes 4 (½-cup) servings

NUTRITION AT A GLANCE
Per serving: 30 calories, 0 g fat, 0 g saturated fat, 1 g protein, 7 g carbohydrate, 1 g fiber, 150 mg sodium

Southern-Style Greens

PREP TIME: 10 minutes   **COOK TIME:** 15 minutes

A few slices of smoky turkey bacon turn simple kale into a scrumptious Southern favorite that's perfect with any grilled or baked fish or meat (especially if it's got a little kick!).

2 teaspoons extra-virgin olive oil

3 slices turkey bacon, finely chopped

1 small onion, finely chopped

2 garlic cloves, minced

1 cup water

1 (1-pound) bunch kale, stemmed and thinly sliced (8 cups)

¼ teaspoon salt

⅛ teaspoon freshly ground black pepper

In a large nonstick skillet, heat oil over medium heat. Add bacon and cook until browned and crisp, 3 to 5 minutes. Remove bacon from the skillet with a slotted spoon and drain on paper towels.

Add onion and garlic to the skillet and cook, stirring occasionally, over medium heat until onion is softened, about 3 minutes. Add water and half of the kale; bring to a simmer, cover, and cook until kale is wilted, about 2 minutes. Add remaining kale, salt, and pepper; cover and cook until kale is tender and water has evaporated, about 3 minutes more.

Add bacon to the skillet; stir to combine with kale and heat through, about 30 seconds. Divide among 4 plates and serve warm.

Makes 4 (1-cup) servings

NUTRITION AT A GLANCE
Per serving: 110 calories, 5 g fat, 1 g saturated fat, 5 g protein, 12 g carbohydrate, 2 g fiber, 330 mg sodium

Spicy Grilled Sweet Potato Fries

PREP TIME: 15 minutes   **COOK TIME:** 10 minutes

Paprika partners with thyme, black pepper, and cayenne to spice up these tasty grilled fries that are far healthier than their deep-fried counterparts. Cut them extra thin, and be sure to use a grill topper or vegetable basket. In cooler months, you can bake the fries in a hot oven.

- 4 medium sweet potatoes (about 1 pound), peeled
- 2 tablespoons extra-virgin olive oil
- 1 teaspoon paprika
- 1 teaspoon dried thyme
- ¼ teaspoon salt
- ¼ teaspoon cayenne
- ⅛ teaspoon freshly ground black pepper

Lightly coat a grill or grill pan with cooking spray and heat to medium-high.

Cut sweet potatoes into fries ⅓ inch thick by 2 to 4 inches long. In a medium bowl, combine sweet potatoes, oil, paprika, thyme, salt, cayenne, and black pepper. Grill sweet potatoes, turning occasionally, until tender and lightly browned, 8 to 10 minutes. Transfer to a platter and serve hot.

Makes 4 (1-cup) servings

NUTRITION AT A GLANCE
Per serving: 200 calories, 7 g fat, 1 g saturated fat, 2 g protein, 32 g carbohydrate, 4 g fiber, 190 mg sodium

Savoy Slaw with Sesame Dressing

PREP TIME: 10 minutes   **COOK TIME:** 5 minutes

Frilly Savoy cabbage, used frequently in Asian cooking, is available in the produce section of most supermarkets. Its mellow flavor makes it ideal for salads and slaws. As with all cabbages, it offers vitamin C, fiber, and health-giving phytonutrients.

- 1 tablespoon sesame seeds
- 1 (1½-pound) Savoy cabbage, shredded (4 cups)
- 1 medium red bell pepper, cut into thin strips
- 1 tablespoon toasted sesame oil
- 2 teaspoons red wine vinegar
- ¼ teaspoon salt
- ⅛ teaspoon freshly ground black pepper

In a small skillet, toast sesame seeds over medium–low heat, shaking the pan occasionally, until seeds are golden, about 5 minutes. Remove from the heat.

In a large bowl, combine cabbage, bell pepper, sesame oil, vinegar, salt, and black pepper. Add sesame seeds and toss. Serve at room temperature.

Makes 4 (generous ¾-cup) servings

NUTRITION AT A GLANCE
Per serving: 70 calories, 4.5 g fat, 0.5 g saturated fat, 2 g protein, 7 g carbohydrate, 3 g fiber, 166 mg sodium

Spanish Rice Salad with Pumpkin Seeds

PREP TIME: 15 minutes   **COOK TIME:** 15 minutes   **CHILL TIME:** 5 minutes

This delicious rice uses classic Spanish ingredients like green olives, pumpkin seeds, and sherry vinegar to create a perfect accompaniment for simple grilled fish, chicken, or meat dishes. Try it with Grilled Tuna with Provençal Anchovy Sauce (page 108), Garlicky Chicken Skewers (page 129), or Pork Pinchos with Shredded Cabbage Salad (page 160). You can use roasted pumpkin seeds, if desired.

- ½ cup quick-cooking whole-grain brown rice
- 2 medium tomatoes, finely chopped
- 1 small onion, finely chopped
- ½ cup pitted green olives, sliced lengthwise
- ¼ cup pumpkin seeds
- 1 tablespoon extra-virgin olive oil
- 1 teaspoon sherry vinegar
- 1 teaspoon dried oregano
- ¼ teaspoon salt
- ⅛ teaspoon freshly ground black pepper
- 2 tablespoons chopped fresh parsley

Cook rice according to package directions. Remove from the heat, spread on a plate, and refrigerate until cooled to room temperature, about 5 minutes.

In a large bowl, combine rice, tomatoes, onion, olives, pumpkin seeds, oil, vinegar, oregano, salt, and pepper. Divide salad among 4 plates and sprinkle with parsley just before serving.

Makes 4 (¾-cup) servings

NUTRITION AT A GLANCE
Per serving: 170 calories, 7 g fat, 0.5 g saturated fat, 4 g protein, 25 g carbohydrate, 3 g fiber, 240 mg sodium

Green Rice with Summer Peas

PREP TIME: 20 minutes   **COOK TIME:** 20 minutes

A blend of fragrant and flavorful fresh herbs gives this tasty, versatile side its vibrant color and taste. If you don't have all of the herbs, simply use more of the ones you do have.

½ cup quick-cooking whole-grain brown rice

2 tablespoons water

1 tablespoon plus 2 teaspoons extra-virgin olive oil

1 tablespoon chopped fresh basil

1 tablespoon chopped fresh parsley

2 teaspoons chopped fresh mint

2 teaspoons chopped fresh tarragon

2 scallions, finely chopped

1 cup snow peas, trimmed

¾ cup fresh or frozen peas

¼ teaspoon salt

Freshly ground black pepper

Cook rice according to package directions. Remove from the heat and keep warm.

While rice is cooking, in a blender combine water, 1 tablespoon of the oil, basil, parsley, mint, and tarragon; purée until smooth.

In a large nonstick skillet, heat remaining 2 teaspoons oil over medium heat. Add scallions and cook until fragrant, about 1 minute. Add snow peas and regular peas and cook 2 minutes more. Add cooked rice and stir well to combine and heat through, about 1 minute more.

Remove rice mixture from the heat, transfer to a serving bowl, and stir in herb mixture, salt, and pepper to taste. Serve warm or at room temperature.

Makes 4 (¾-cup) servings

NUTRITION AT A GLANCE
Per serving: 120 calories, 7 g fat, 1 g saturated fat, 3 g protein, 13 g carbohydrate, 2 g fiber, 150 mg sodium

Red Beans and Rice

PREP TIME: 10 minutes   **COOK TIME:** 20 minutes

This traditional Louisiana side dish makes a great partner for Grilled Steak with Texas Mop Sauce (page 163) or Jerk Chicken with Cool Romaine Salad (page 144).

½   cup quick-cooking whole-grain brown rice

1   tablespoon extra-virgin olive oil

1   onion, finely chopped

1   (15-ounce) can red kidney beans, rinsed and drained

½   teaspoon dried thyme

¼   teaspoon garlic powder

¼   teaspoon hot pepper sauce, or more to taste

¼   teaspoon salt

⅛   teaspoon freshly ground black pepper

⅛   teaspoon ground white pepper

Cook rice according to package directions. Remove from the heat.

In a large nonstick skillet, heat oil over medium heat. Add onion and cook until translucent and beginning to brown, 3 to 5 minutes. Add rice, beans, thyme, garlic powder, hot pepper sauce, salt, black pepper, and white pepper; stir to combine. Cook until heated through, about 2 minutes. Serve hot.

Makes 4 (¾-cup) servings

NUTRITION AT A GLANCE
Per serving: 140 calories, 4.5 g fat, 0.5 g saturated fat, 5 g protein, 20 g carbohydrate, 4 g fiber, 400 mg sodium

Citrusy Hot Pepper Slaw

PREP TIME: 20 minutes

For the crispest salad, serve this slaw soon after it's made. For a slightly wilted version, let it sit at room temperature for 10 to 15 minutes. You can also refrigerate it overnight and serve chilled, if desired.

- 1 large seedless orange
- ½ (3-pound) green cabbage, shredded (6 cups)
- 2 medium jalapeños, seeded and minced
- 1 tablespoon fresh lemon juice
- 1 tablespoon extra-virgin olive oil
- ¼ teaspoon salt
- ⅛ teaspoon freshly ground black pepper

Finely grate zest from half of the orange over a medium bowl; set aside. Peel orange. Holding orange over a small bowl to catch juice, carefully cut along the membrane on both sides of each orange segment. Allow the freed segments to fall into the bowl.

Squeeze the remaining membrane over the bowl containing zest to extract any additional juice. Pour any juice from orange segments into the bowl with zest. Roughly chop orange segments and add them to the bowl with zest and juice.

Add cabbage, jalapeños, lemon juice, oil, salt, and pepper to the bowl with the orange; toss well. Serve at room temperature.

Makes 4 (generous 1-cup) servings

NUTRITION AT A GLANCE
Per serving: 80 calories, 3.5 g fat, 0.5 g saturated fat, 2 g protein, 12 g carbohydrate, 4 g fiber, 160 mg sodium

FRESH FROM THE SEA

From mild and sweet to richer-tasting varieties, fish and shellfish offer a wide array of fantastic flavors and nutrients. All fish provide high-quality lean protein and important vitamins and minerals, such as B vitamins, calcium, and iron. And the more oily types like salmon, Spanish mackerel, anchovies, and sardines supply the highest amounts of beneficial heart-healthy omega-3 fatty acids. Before you head for the fish market, however, be aware that certain species, such as king mackerel, tilefish, and swordfish, can be high in mercury and/or other contaminants and should be avoided.

A natural match for the grill, seafood is a perfect fit for warm-weather dining. In the pages ahead, you'll find a host of mouth-watering grilling options, including whole fish, fish burgers, seafood kebabs, and tacos. And for days when you want to broil, poach, or pan-cook, you'll have your pick of dishes like Southern-Style Shrimp Boil, Seafood Paella (with shrimp, clams, and mussels), Crab and Shrimp Cakes with Caper Sauce, Fresh Blackened Tuna with Greens, and more.

◀ *Southern-Style Shrimp Boil (page 96)*

Southern-Style Shrimp Boil

PREP TIME: 15 minutes   **COOK TIME:** 20 minutes

Hot Italian turkey sausage is now widely available in low-fat versions. It spices up this dish, which is almost as much fun to make as it is to eat. Give diners plenty of napkins and empty bowls for the shrimp shells. Or line the picnic table with newspapers and enjoy this dish outdoors. For Phases 1 and 2, omit the corn.

- 2 tablespoons shrimp boil seasoning or crab boil seasoning
- 1 (4-ounce) low-fat hot Italian turkey sausage link, casing removed and sausage crumbled
- 2 ears of corn, shucked, each cut into 4 pieces
- 1 small red onion, cut into thin wedges
- 4 ounces green beans, trimmed and halved
- 1½ pounds large unpeeled shrimp

Fill a large saucepan with water to three-quarters full, add shrimp boil seasoning, and bring to a boil. Add sausage, corn, onion, and green beans; return to a simmer and cook for 5 minutes. Add shrimp, return to a simmer, and cook until shrimp are pink, 2 to 3 minutes more. Drain in a large colander.

Divide shrimp boil among 4 shallow bowls and serve warm.

Makes 4 servings

NUTRITION AT A GLANCE
Per serving with corn: 250 calories, 5 g fat, 1 g saturated fat, 38 g protein, 13 g carbohydrate, 2 g fiber, 630 mg sodium
Per serving without corn: 207 calories, 4 g fat, 1 g saturated fat, 36 g protein, 5 g carbohydrate, 1 g fiber, 630 mg sodium

Fresh Blackened Tuna with Greens

PREP TIME: 5 minutes   **COOK TIME:** 8 minutes

Cajun seasoning adds beaucoup flavor to this Southern-style dish. You'll find many commercial Cajun seasoning blends—typically containing salt, cayenne, paprika, black and white pepper, and onion and garlic powder—in the spice section of your supermarket. Try arugula or spinach in place of the mixed baby greens, if you like.

4   (6-ounce) tuna steaks or fillets, about 1¼ inches thick

1   tablespoon Cajun seasoning

1   tablespoon extra-virgin olive oil

1   teaspoon grated lemon zest

2   teaspoons fresh lemon juice

6   ounces mixed baby greens (6 cups)

   Salt and freshly ground black pepper

Lightly coat a large cast-iron skillet with cooking spray and heat over medium-high heat. Rub each side of the tuna steaks with Cajun seasoning. Place steaks in the pan and cook until blackened, but not burned, on each side, about 3 minutes per side for medium-rare. Remove the pan from the heat.

In a large bowl, whisk together oil, lemon zest, and lemon juice. Add greens and toss to coat. Season with salt and pepper to taste and divide salad among 4 plates. Top each with a piece of blackened tuna and serve.

Makes 4 servings

NUTRITION AT A GLANCE
Per serving: 230 calories, 5 g fat, 1 g saturated fat, 41 g protein, 4 g carbohydrate, 2 g fiber, 500 mg sodium

Lemony Poached Halibut with Creamy Cucumbers

PREP TIME: 20 minutes   **COOK TIME: 15 minutes**

Combining cucumber with reduced-fat sour cream and dill creates a smooth and creamy sauce that's a perfect foil for mild-tasting halibut. If you're on Phase 2 or 3, make a halibut sandwich with any leftover fish: Flake the halibut with a fork and stuff it into a whole-grain pita half with the cucumber sauce, some shredded lettuce, and an extra squeeze of lemon.

4   cups water

2   lemons, thinly sliced

3   medium shallots, thinly sliced

4   (6-ounce) pieces halibut fillet, skin removed

2   medium cucumbers, thinly sliced

3   tablespoons roughly chopped fresh dill

¼   cup reduced-fat sour cream

¼   teaspoon salt

In a medium saucepan, bring water, lemons, and shallots to a simmer over medium-high heat. Add halibut, nestling fish pieces under lemons and shallots. Return water to a simmer and simmer gently until fish is opaque and tender, 5 to 8 minutes.

While fish is cooking, in a medium bowl combine cucumbers, dill, sour cream, and salt.

When fish is done, using a large slotted spoon, carefully transfer fish to 4 plates. Drain lemon and shallot slices and place on top of fish. Serve warm with cucumbers on the side.

Makes 4 servings

NUTRITION AT A GLANCE
Per serving: 230 calories, 6 g fat, 1.5 g saturated fat, 37 g protein, 7 g carbohydrate, 2 g fiber, 250 mg sodium

Seafood Paella

PREP TIME: 25 minutes   **COOK TIME:** 25 minutes

Red peppers add extra flavor and vibrant color to this elegant but easy Spanish dish. Do as the Spaniards do and use zesty roasted piquillo peppers. You can find them jarred in larger supermarkets and specialty stores. See page 115 for directions for cleaning mussels.

- 1 tablespoon extra-virgin olive oil
- 1 (4-ounce) low-fat hot Italian turkey sausage link
- 1 medium onion, chopped
- 2 garlic cloves, sliced
- ⅓ cup white wine
- 1 cup quick-cooking whole-grain brown rice
- 1½ cups lower-sodium chicken broth
- 2 roasted red peppers (from a jar), thinly sliced

- Pinch saffron
- ½ pound large shrimp, peeled and deveined
- 2 large plum tomatoes, chopped
- ½ cup fresh or frozen baby peas
- 1½ pounds littleneck clams or cockles (about 2 dozen), cleaned
- 1½ pounds mussels (about 2 dozen), cleaned
- Freshly ground black pepper

In a large saucepan, heat oil over medium heat. Add sausage and cook until browned on all sides, about 5 minutes; transfer to a cutting board. Add onion and garlic to the pan; cook over medium heat until softened, about 5 minutes.

Meanwhile, cut sausage into thin slices. Return sausage to the pan and add wine, scraping up any browned bits from the bottom of the pan. Add rice, broth, red peppers, and saffron; bring to a simmer, cover, and cook for 5 minutes.

Stir in shrimp, tomatoes, and peas. Add clams and mussels, cover, and cook until clams and mussels open, about 5 minutes. Discard any shellfish that haven't opened. Season lightly with black pepper. Divide among 4 bowls and serve warm.

Makes 4 servings

NUTRITION AT A GLANCE
Per serving: 320 calories, 9 g fat, 1.5 g saturated fat, 34 g protein, 23 g carbohydrate, 2 g fiber, 710 mg sodium

Crab and Shrimp Cakes with Caper Sauce

PREP TIME: 25 minutes   **COOK TIME:** 15 minutes   **CHILL TIME:** 30 minutes

This is a delicious change of pace from regular crab cakes. The combination of lump crabmeat and shrimp makes it an excellent choice for a special occasion.

Sauce

2 tablespoons capers, rinsed and drained

2 tablespoons mayonnaise

1 tablespoon fresh lemon juice

½ teaspoon Dijon mustard

Cakes

3 teaspoons extra-virgin olive oil

½ pound large shrimp, peeled and deveined

1 medium yellow or red bell pepper, finely chopped

2 medium shallots, finely chopped

1 pound fresh lump crabmeat

1 large egg

2 tablespoons finely chopped chives

1 teaspoon Dijon mustard

For the sauce: In a food processor, combine capers, mayonnaise, lemon juice, and mustard; pulse until capers are very finely chopped. Transfer to an airtight container and refrigerate until ready to use.

For the cakes: In a large nonstick skillet, heat 1½ teaspoons of the oil over high heat. Add shrimp and cook until pink, about 1 minute per side; transfer to a plate to cool. Add pepper and shallots to the skillet and reduce the heat to medium; cook, stirring frequently, until just beginning to soften, about 2 minutes. Transfer to a medium bowl.

Place cooled shrimp in the food processor and pulse until finely chopped. Add to the bowl with pepper and shallots. Add crab, egg, chives, and mustard to shrimp mixture; stir well. Form mixture into 8 cakes, 1 inch thick. Transfer to a plate, cover with plastic wrap, and refrigerate for 30 minutes.

In the same large nonstick skillet, heat remaining 1½ teaspoons oil over medium heat. Add cakes and cook until golden on the outside and warmed through, about 4 minutes per side (turn carefully). Divide among 4 plates and serve warm, topped with caper sauce.

Makes 4 (2-cake) servings

NUTRITION AT A GLANCE
Per serving: 270 calories, 12 g fat, 2 g saturated fat, 36 g protein, 3 g carbohydrate, 0 g fiber, 700 mg sodium

Grilled Fish Tacos with Spicy Melon Salsa

PREP TIME: 15 minutes   **COOK TIME:** 12 minutes

Sea bass is well suited for this tasty taco because its mild flavor complements the sweet melon, zippy lime, and spicy jalapeño pepper in the salsa. You can use halibut or scallops instead, if you prefer.

- 3 tablespoons fresh lime juice
- 3 teaspoons extra-virgin olive oil
- 1 pound skinless sea bass fillets
- ¼ teaspoon salt
  Freshly ground black pepper
- 2 cups finely chopped cantaloupe (about 2½-pound melon)
- ¼ cup chopped fresh cilantro
- 2 scallions, thinly sliced
- 1 jalapeño, seeded and minced
- 2 (10-inch) whole-wheat tortillas
- 1 lime, cut into wedges

In a 9- by 13-inch glass baking dish, whisk together 1 tablespoon of the lime juice and 1 teaspoon of the oil. Add fish and turn to coat. Sprinkle with salt and season lightly with black pepper.

Lightly coat a grill or grill pan with cooking spray and heat to medium-high. Grill fish until opaque and tender, about 5 minutes per side. Transfer fish to a cutting board and cut into 1-inch chunks.

In a small bowl, combine cantaloupe, cilantro, scallions, jalapeño, remaining 2 tablespoons lime juice, and remaining 2 teaspoons oil.

Grill tortillas until warm, about 30 seconds per side. Cut each into 4 quarters. Divide fish among tortillas, top with melon salsa, and serve warm with lime wedges.

Makes 4 (2-piece) servings

NUTRITION AT A GLANCE
Per serving: 231 calories, 7 g fat, 1 g saturated fat, 23 g protein, 19 g carbohydrate, 3 g fiber, 353 mg sodium

Warm Shrimp and Penne with Dill

PREP TIME: 20 minutes   **COOK TIME:** 30 minutes

Great served warm or at room temperature, this dish is ideal picnic fare for the backyard or beach. Use any small, shaped pasta you have on hand. For a smoky flavor, grill the shrimp and scallions (this can be done up to 1 day ahead).

1 pound large shrimp, peeled and deveined

8 ounces whole-wheat penne

1 cup grape tomatoes, halved

½ cup low-fat or nonfat plain yogurt

3 scallions, finely sliced

2 tablespoons chopped fresh dill

1 tablespoon capers, rinsed, drained, and chopped

2 teaspoons finely grated lemon zest

¼ teaspoon salt

¼ teaspoon freshly ground black pepper

Bring a large saucepan of water to a boil. Add shrimp, return to a simmer, and cook until shrimp turn pink, 1 to 2 minutes. Using a slotted spoon, transfer shrimp to a large bowl; keep water boiling over high heat.

Add pasta to boiling water and cook according to package directions until al dente. Drain (do not rinse) and add to the bowl with shrimp.

Add tomatoes, yogurt, scallions, dill, capers, lemon zest, salt, and pepper to the bowl with pasta and shrimp; toss well. Serve warm.

Makes 4 (2-cup) servings

NUTRITION AT A GLANCE
Per serving: 330 calories, 3.5 g fat, 0 g saturated fat, 28 g protein, 46 g carbohydrate, 6 g fiber, 370 mg sodium

Grilled Salmon and Farro Salad

PREP TIME: 10 minutes   COOK TIME: 40 minutes

Rich in fiber, protein, and B vitamins, farro is an ancient relative of wheat, with a hearty texture and a delicious nutlike flavor. Look for it in larger supermarkets, Italian markets, and specialty food shops. Barley or spelt make good substitutes.

½ cup farro

1 pound salmon fillet (about ¾ inch thick), skin removed

3 teaspoons extra-virgin olive oil

Freshly ground black pepper

¼ cup finely chopped fresh parsley

3 scallions, thinly sliced

1 tablespoon grated orange zest

2 teaspoons fresh lemon juice

¼ teaspoon salt

4 large red leaf lettuce leaves

Bring a medium saucepan of water to a boil, add farro, and cook until tender, 25 to 30 minutes. Drain (do not rinse) and transfer to a large bowl.

While farro is cooking, lightly coat a grill or grill pan with cooking spray and heat to medium–high. Brush salmon with 1 teaspoon of the oil and season lightly with pepper. Grill salmon until it can be flaked with a fork, 4 to 5 minutes per side. Transfer to a cutting board; when cool enough to handle, flake with a fork into the bowl with farro.

Add parsley, scallions, orange zest, lemon juice, salt, and remaining 2 teaspoons oil to farro and salmon; toss well. Season with pepper to taste. Divide lettuce among 4 plates, top with farro mixture, and serve warm or at room temperature.

Makes 4 (1-cup) servings

NUTRITION AT A GLANCE
Per serving: 350 calories, 17 g fat, 3 g saturated fat, 27 g protein, 23 g carbohydrate, 6 g fiber, 220 mg sodium

Seared Scallops with Summer Vegetables

PREP TIME: 20 minutes   **COOK TIME:** 20 minutes

Sweet and delicious, scallops sometimes come with a "foot" attached; this small tough muscle pulls away easily and should be removed. To enjoy this recipe on Phase 1 or 2, simply omit the corn.

4	teaspoons extra-virgin olive oil
1½	pounds sea scallops (about 20), cleaned
¼	teaspoon salt
	Freshly ground black pepper
1	medium zucchini, halved lengthwise and thinly sliced into half-moons
½	small onion, finely chopped
2	garlic cloves, minced
1	cup cherry tomatoes, halved
¾	cup frozen shelled edamame, defrosted
1	small ear of corn, shucked, kernels sliced off cob (½ cup kernels)
2	tablespoons chopped fresh basil

In a large nonstick skillet, heat 2 teaspoons of the oil over medium–high heat. Add scallops, sprinkle with ⅛ teaspoon of the salt, and season lightly with pepper. Cook until golden brown on the outside and opaque inside, about 2 to 3 minutes per side. Transfer to a plate and keep warm.

Reduce the heat to medium and add remaining 2 teaspoons oil to the pan. Add zucchini, onion, and garlic; cook until vegetables are softened, about 5 minutes. Add tomatoes, edamame, and corn; cook until tomatoes begin to break down, 3 to 4 minutes. Return scallops to the pan and sprinkle with remaining ⅛ teaspoon salt and pepper to taste; reheat for 30 seconds, or until heated through. Stir in basil. Divide among 4 plates and serve warm.

Makes 4 servings

NUTRITION AT A GLANCE

Per serving with corn: 180 calories, 8 g fat, 1 g saturated fat, 18 g protein, 11 g carbohydrate, 2 g fiber, 280 mg sodium

Per serving without corn: 161 calories, 7 g fat, 1 g saturated fat, 17 g protein, 7 g carbohydrate, 1 g fiber, 274 mg sodium

Grilled Tuna with Provençal Anchovy Sauce

PREP TIME: 5 minutes   **COOK TIME: 10 minutes**

This simple recipe is made with herbes de Provence, a dried herb blend that is used regularly in southern France and most often includes basil, fennel seed, lavender, marjoram, summer savory, rosemary, and thyme. If you can't find it in the spice section of your supermarket, mix up your own with a dried assortment from your pantry and keep it in a jar with the other spices. You don't need all of the herbs to make a great blend.

- 1½ pounds tuna steaks, about 1¼ inches thick
- 1 tablespoon extra-virgin olive oil
- 1 small garlic clove, minced
- ½ teaspoon herbes de Provence
- 2 anchovy fillets
- 1 tablespoon red wine vinegar
- 1 tablespoon chopped fresh parsley

Lightly coat a grill or grill pan with cooking spray and heat to medium-high. Grill tuna 2 to 3 minutes per side for medium-rare. Transfer to a cutting board.

In a small saucepan, heat oil over medium-low heat. Add garlic and cook, stirring with a wooden spoon, until softened but not browned, about 1 minute. Add herbes de Provence and anchovies, mashing anchovies with the back of the wooden spoon until they break up, about 30 seconds. Remove the pan from the heat and stir in vinegar and parsley. Transfer anchovy sauce to a small bowl.

Thinly slice tuna, divide among 4 plates, and drizzle with anchovy sauce. Serve warm.

Makes 4 servings

NUTRITION AT A GLANCE
Per serving: 220 calories, 5 g fat, 1 g saturated fat, 40 g protein, 0 g carbohydrate, 0 g fiber, 105 mg sodium

Mixed Seafood Kebabs with Parsley-Garlic Sauce

PREP TIME: 30 minutes   **COOK TIME:** 20 minutes

These fresh seafood skewers, slathered with a delicious Mediterranean-style sauce, seem to taste even better when enjoyed outdoors with friends and family. Serve them with a large green salad and you have an easy summer meal. Let your fish purveyor skin the halibut for you, or use halibut steaks instead.

Sauce

- 2 large garlic cloves, minced
- 1½ tablespoons finely chopped fresh parsley
- 1 tablespoon extra-virgin olive oil
- 1 tablespoon fresh lemon juice
- ¼ teaspoon salt

Kebabs

- 1 pound sea scallops (about 16), cleaned
- 1 pound halibut fillet (about 1¼ inches thick), skin removed, fish cut into 1½-inch pieces
- 1 large zucchini, cut into ½-inch-thick rounds
- 1 small red onion, cut into ½-inch-thick wedges
- ¼ teaspoon freshly ground black pepper

Special equipment

- 8 (12-inch) skewers

For the sauce: Place garlic in a small saucepan and add water just to cover. Bring to a boil, reduce the heat, and simmer for 5 minutes; strain and transfer garlic to a small bowl. Add parsley, oil, lemon juice, and salt to garlic; stir to combine.

For the kebabs: Thread scallops, halibut, zucchini, and onion alternately onto skewers; season with pepper.

Generously coat a grill or grill pan with cooking spray and heat to medium-high. Grill kebabs, turning once, until fish is cooked through and vegetables are lightly charred, 10 to 12 minutes. Serve warm or at room temperature, drizzled with parsley–garlic sauce.

Makes 4 (2-skewer) servings

NUTRITION AT A GLANCE

Per serving: 280 calories, 7 g fat, 1 g saturated fat, 44 g protein, 8 g carbohydrate, 1 g fiber, 400 mg sodium

Pasta with Salmon, Peas, Mint, and Feta

PREP TIME: 15 minutes   COOK TIME: 20 minutes

Peas and fresh mint are a summertime classic. Add grilled salmon and a sprinkling of feta cheese and you have the makings for this heavenly pasta dish. For the photo, opposite, we used whole-wheat chiocciole, which looks like a seashell, but you can use any shaped whole-wheat pasta you like.

- 1   pound salmon fillet (about 1 inch thick), skin removed
- 1   (8-ounce) package shaped whole-wheat pasta
- 1   cup fresh or frozen baby peas
- 2   ounces crumbled reduced-fat feta cheese (⅓ cup)
- ¼   cup chopped fresh mint, plus mint leaves for garnish
- 2   tablespoons fresh lemon juice
- ¼   teaspoon salt

Heat the broiler. Cover a broiler pan with foil and lightly coat with cooking spray. Place salmon on the broiler pan and broil until fish is opaque and cooked through, about 10 minutes. Remove salmon from the broiler and transfer to a large bowl. When cool enough to handle, cut into bite-size pieces.

While salmon is cooking, bring a large saucepan of lightly salted water to a boil. Cook pasta according to package directions until al dente, adding peas during the last 2 minutes of cooking. Reserving ¼ cup of the pasta cooking water, drain pasta and peas and transfer to the bowl with salmon.

In a medium bowl, whisk together feta, mint, lemon juice, salt, and reserved ¼ cup pasta cooking water to make a sauce. Pour sauce over pasta and salmon and toss gently to coat. Serve warm.

Makes 4 (generous 1½-cup) servings

NUTRITION AT A GLANCE
Per serving: 460 calories, 15 g fat, 3.5 g saturated fat, 36 g protein, 49 g carbohydrate, 9 g fiber, 440 mg sodium

Spicy BBQ Shrimp and Rice

PREP TIME: 25 minutes   COOK TIME: 20 minutes

This finger-licking-good shrimp is a staple of summer cooking in the American South. It can easily be enjoyed on Phase 1; just skip the rice and serve the shrimp with a salad instead.

Rice

- 1 tablespoon extra-virgin olive oil
- 3 scallions, white and green parts thinly sliced and kept separate
- 1 medium green bell pepper, finely chopped
- 1 cup quick-cooking whole-grain brown rice
- 1¾ cups water

Shrimp

- 1 tablespoon extra-virgin olive oil
- 1 tablespoon paprika
- 1 teaspoon garlic powder
- ½ teaspoon dried thyme
- 4 scallions, thinly sliced
- 1 tablespoon fresh lemon juice
- 1 tablespoon Worcestershire sauce
- ¾ cup tomato sauce
- 2 tablespoons granular sugar substitute
- 2 teaspoons hot pepper sauce
- 2 pounds large shrimp, peeled and deveined

For the rice: In a large nonstick saucepan, heat oil over medium heat. Add scallion whites and pepper; cook, stirring, until vegetables just begin to soften, about 5 minutes. Add rice and stir to coat. Add water, cover, and cook rice according to package directions.

For the shrimp: While rice is cooking, in a large nonstick skillet heat oil over medium heat. Add paprika, garlic powder, and thyme; cook, stirring, until fragrant, about 1 minute. Stir in scallions, lemon juice, Worcestershire sauce, tomato sauce, sugar substitute, and hot pepper sauce; cook 1 minute more. Add shrimp and toss to coat with sauce; cover and cook 2 to 3 minutes, or until shrimp turn pink. Remove from the heat and keep warm.

To serve, divide rice among 4 plates, top with shrimp, and sprinkle with scallion greens.

Makes 4 servings

NUTRITION AT A GLANCE
Per serving: 370 calories, 12 g fat, 2 g saturated fat, 43 g protein, 22 g carbohydrate, 3 g fiber, 580 mg sodium

Lemon-Grilled Whole Trout with Pesto

PREP TIME: 10 minutes   **COOK TIME:** 10 minutes

Fresh trout—with its mild, delicate, and sweet taste—is perfect for grilling, broiling, or roasting whole. Common small varieties include brook, golden, and rainbow. Use a fish-shaped grill basket for easy turning. If you have a lot of basil on hand and prefer to make your own pesto, see page 13.

4   whole trout (about 12 ounces each), cleaned and boned

1   tablespoon extra-virgin olive oil

¼   teaspoon salt

   Freshly ground black pepper

3   lemons

2   tablespoons store-bought pesto

Lightly coat the outside of each trout with oil. Sprinkle evenly inside and out with salt and season lightly with pepper. Slice 2 of the lemons into 8 slices each. Place 4 slices, slightly overlapping, inside the cavity of each fish. Cut remaining lemon into wedges.

Lightly coat a grill or grill pan with cooking spray and heat to medium-high. Grill fish until lightly browned on the outside and opaque and tender inside, about 5 minutes per side. Remove from the grill and remove heads and tails, if desired. Remove and discard lemon slices.

Place fish on 4 serving plates, gently open each, flesh side up, and spread 1½ teaspoons pesto on the inside of each fish. Serve warm with lemon wedges.

Makes 4 servings

NUTRITION AT A GLANCE
Per serving: 280 calories, 13 g fat, 2.5 g saturated fat, 36 g protein, 1 g carbohydrate, 0 g fiber, 260 mg sodium

Steamed Mussels with Garden Vegetable Broth

PREP TIME: 20 minutes   COOK TIME: 10 minutes

In the summertime, mussels are especially good steamed in a broth filled with garden-fresh vegetables. Toss in extra herbs of your choice. To clean mussels before cooking, run them under cold water, scrubbing gently with a vegetable brush. Discard any with broken shells and those with shells that remain open after being tapped. Also pull off and discard the weedy "beard" that is sometimes attached to the shell.

- 1 tablespoon extra-virgin olive oil
- 1 medium zucchini, cut into ½-inch pieces
- 2 scallions, white and green parts thinly sliced and kept separate
- 2 medium plum tomatoes, cut into ½-inch cubes
- ⅓ cup white wine
- 2 garlic cloves, minced
- 4 pounds mussels, cleaned
- 2 tablespoons thinly sliced fresh basil

In a large nonstick saucepan, heat oil over medium–high heat. Add zucchini and scallion whites; cook, stirring, until zucchini begins to brown, about 3 minutes. Stir in tomatoes, wine, and garlic; bring to a simmer. Add mussels, stir, and cover. Steam mussels until they open, about 5 minutes, gently stirring halfway through cooking. Discard any mussels that haven't opened.

Divide mussels, broth, and vegetables among 4 bowls. Sprinkle with scallion greens and basil; serve hot.

Makes 4 servings

NUTRITION AT A GLANCE
Per serving: 190 calories, 7 g fat, 1 g saturated fat, 18 g protein, 10 g carbohydrate, 2 g fiber, 400 mg sodium

Asian Tuna Burgers

PREP TIME: 10 minutes   **COOK TIME:** 11 minutes

Wasabi, or Japanese horseradish, can be purchased as a paste (in a tube) or as a powder (just reconstitute the powder with a little water to form a paste) in the Asian section of most supermarkets. Here the wasabi is blended with sour cream and lemon juice to make a spicy sauce for these fresh tuna burgers. Skip the bun if you're on Phase 1.

- 1 tablespoon sesame seeds
- 1 pound fresh tuna, cut into 1-inch chunks
- 2 scallions, coarsely chopped
- 1 tablespoon Dijon mustard
- 2 teaspoons toasted sesame oil
- 1½ teaspoons low-sodium soy sauce
- 2 tablespoons reduced-fat sour cream
- ½ teaspoon fresh lemon juice
- ¼ teaspoon wasabi paste
- 4 whole-wheat or whole-grain buns, lightly toasted (optional)

In a small skillet, toast sesame seeds over medium-low heat, shaking the pan back and forth until seeds are golden, about 5 minutes. Transfer to a plate to cool.

In a food processor, combine tuna, scallions, mustard, sesame oil, soy sauce, and sesame seeds. Pulse just until mixture comes together (it should not be finely ground), 15 to 20 seconds. Form mixture into 4 patties, about ¾ inch thick.

In a small bowl, whisk together sour cream, lemon juice, and wasabi.

Lightly coat a grill or grill pan with cooking spray and heat to medium-high. Grill patties 2 to 3 minutes per side for medium-rare. Place burgers on buns, if using; top each burger with wasabi sauce and serve.

Makes 4 servings

NUTRITION AT A GLANCE
Per serving with bun: 330 calories, 12 g fat, 3 g saturated fat, 31 g protein, 24 g carbohydrate, 4 g fiber, 440 mg sodium
Per serving without bun: 220 calories, 10 g fat, 2.5 g saturated fat, 28 g protein, 2 g carbohydrate, 2 g fiber, 230 mg sodium

South-of-the-Border Salmon Burgers

PREP TIME: 15 minutes   COOK TIME: 12 minutes

Salmon's rich meat is perfect for making tasty, well-formed patties. Chili powder, cumin, lime, and cilantro create a Tex-Mex flavor here. For a Greek variation, try chopped fresh oregano, thyme, minced onion, and garlic. For Phase 2, serve the burgers in whole-wheat pitas.

1 pound salmon fillet, skin removed, fish cut into 1-inch chunks	1 (8-ounce) head romaine, shredded (4 cups)
2 teaspoons plus ¼ cup reduced-fat sour cream	1 medium avocado, cubed
1½ teaspoons Dijon mustard	2 teaspoons extra-virgin olive oil
1 teaspoon chili powder	2 teaspoons fresh lime juice
½ teaspoon ground cumin	1 tablespoon chopped fresh cilantro
¼ teaspoon salt	½ teaspoon cayenne
Freshly ground black pepper	

In a food processor, combine salmon, 2 teaspoons of the sour cream, mustard, chili powder, cumin, ⅛ teaspoon of the salt, and ⅛ teaspoon black pepper; pulse just until mixture comes together, 15 to 20 seconds. Form mixture into 4 patties, about ¾ inch thick.

Lightly coat a grill or grill pan with cooking spray and heat to medium-high. Grill patties until cooked through, 4 to 5 minutes per side.

While patties are cooking, in a large bowl combine lettuce, avocado, oil, 1 teaspoon of the lime juice, and remaining ⅛ teaspoon salt. Season with black pepper to taste.

In a small bowl, whisk together remaining ¼ cup sour cream, remaining 1 teaspoon lime juice, cilantro, and cayenne.

Divide salad among 4 plates and place a burger alongside. Top each burger with a dollop of cilantro sour cream and serve.

Makes 4 servings

NUTRITION AT A GLANCE
Per serving: 330 calories, 23 g fat, 5 g saturated fat, 25 g protein, 6 g carbohydrate, 3 g fiber, 260 mg sodium

Tropical Shrimp and Rice

PREP TIME: 20 minutes   **COOK TIME:** 15 minutes

Toasted shredded coconut and sweet mango bring the taste of the tropics to this flavorful shrimp dish. When purchasing quick-cooking brown rice, be sure to look for brands that are free from partially hydrogenated oils.

- ½ cup quick-cooking whole-grain brown rice
- ¼ cup unsweetened shredded coconut
- 1 pound large shrimp, peeled and deveined
- 1 small mango, peeled and cut into ½-inch cubes
- ¼ cup chopped fresh parsley
- 1 tablespoon extra-virgin olive oil
- 1 teaspoon grated lime zest
- 1 tablespoon fresh lime juice
- ¼ teaspoon salt
- ⅛ teaspoon freshly ground black pepper

Cook rice according to package directions. Transfer to a large bowl to cool.

While rice is cooking, heat the oven to 350°F. Spread coconut on a baking sheet and bake until golden, about 5 minutes. Transfer to a plate to cool.

Bring a saucepan of lightly salted water to a boil. Add shrimp, reduce to a simmer, and cook until shrimp turn pink, 1 to 2 minutes. Transfer shrimp to the bowl with rice.

Add coconut, mango, parsley, oil, lime zest, lime juice, salt, and pepper to shrimp mixture; toss well. Divide shrimp and rice among 4 bowls and serve at room temperature.

Makes 4 (1½-cup) servings

NUTRITION AT A GLANCE
Per serving: 230 calories, 10 g fat, 4 g saturated fat, 21 g protein, 15 g carbohydrate, 2 g fiber, 300 mg sodium

Grilled Spanish Mackerel with Quick Pickled Onions

PREP TIME: 15 minutes   COOK TIME: 25 minutes

Tangy pickled onions are the perfect foil for the rich taste of mackerel—a terrific fish that is high in omega-3 fatty acids and B vitamins. Stick with Spanish mackerel and avoid king mackerel, which has been found to have high mercury levels.

- 1   medium red onion, thinly sliced
- ¼   cup red wine vinegar
- 1   garlic clove, thinly sliced
- 2   teaspoons granular sugar substitute
- Salt
- Freshly ground black pepper
- 4   (6-ounce) Spanish mackerel fillets, with skin
- 1   tablespoon fresh lemon juice
- 1½   teaspoons grated lemon zest
- ½   teaspoon dried oregano

In a small saucepan, combine onion, vinegar, garlic, sugar substitute, salt, and pepper; bring to a simmer, stirring occasionally, and cook until onions are softened and translucent, about 10 minutes. Transfer onions to a serving bowl.

Lightly coat a grill or grill pan with cooking spray and heat to medium-high. Drizzle flesh side of fish evenly with lemon juice and sprinkle with lemon zest and oregano. Lightly season with salt and pepper. Grill fish, skin side down, for 5 minutes; turn and grill 5 to 7 minutes more, or until fish is cooked through and tender.

Divide fish among 4 plates and serve hot with pickled onions on top or on the side.

Makes 4 servings

NUTRITION AT A GLANCE
Per serving: 250 calories, 11 g fat, 3 g saturated fat, 33 g protein, 4 g carbohydrate, 0 g fiber, 250 mg sodium

New England Shellfish Chowder

PREP TIME: 20 minutes   **COOK TIME:** 30 minutes

Chock-full of clams, scallops, and shrimp, along with healthy sweet potato and some bacon for additional flavor—we use lean Canadian, of course—this thick chowder is an East Coast favorite that can easily be doubled for a crowd.

- 1 tablespoon extra-virgin olive oil
- 1 large onion, finely chopped
- 2 celery stalks, finely chopped
- 3 ounces Canadian bacon, cut into ¼-inch cubes
- 1 medium sweet potato (8 ounces), peeled and cut into ½-inch cubes
- 2 (8-ounce) bottles clam juice
- 2 (6½-ounce) cans chopped clams, with liquid
- ¾ pound bay scallops or chopped sea scallops
- ½ pound shrimp, peeled, deveined, and chopped
- 1½ cups 1% milk

  Freshly ground black pepper

In a large nonstick saucepan, heat oil over medium heat. Add onion and celery, cover, and cook until softened, 3 to 5 minutes. Add bacon and cook until lightly browned, about 5 minutes. Add sweet potato and clam juice; bring to a simmer, partially cover, and cook until sweet potato has softened, about 10 minutes.

Stir in clams and their liquid, scallops, shrimp, and milk; return to a simmer and cook, uncovered, until shrimp are pink and scallops are opaque and tender, 3 to 5 minutes. Season lightly with pepper. Divide among 6 bowls and serve hot.

Makes 6 (1½-cup) servings

NUTRITION AT A GLANCE
Per serving: 300 calories, 6 g fat, 1.5 g saturated fat, 39 g protein, 21 g carbohydrate, 2 g fiber, 630 mg sodium

Grilled Shrimp Salad with Chile-Lime Dressing

PREP TIME: 30 minutes **MARINATING TIME:** 30 minutes **COOK TIME:** 10 minutes

You'll impress your guests with this summery salad that has a hint of heat in the marinade and the dressing. For a Phase 1 dish, simply eliminate the papaya.

Shrimp

- 1½ tablespoons extra-virgin olive oil
- 2 teaspoons minced garlic
- ¼ teaspoon crushed red pepper flakes
- 12 to 16 jumbo shrimp (1 to 1½ pounds), peeled and deveined, tails left on
- 4 to 6 scallions, each cut into two (2-inch) pieces

Salad

- 2 tablespoons fresh lime juice
- 2 tablespoons extra-virgin olive oil
- 2 small jalapeños, seeded and minced
- ¼ teaspoon freshly ground black pepper

   Salt

- 4 cups mixed greens, such as frisée, mizuna, radish shoots, and radicchio
- 1 medium papaya, seeded and diced
- 1 medium avocado, thinly sliced
- 1 medium red bell pepper, diced

Special equipment

- 4 (12-inch) skewers

For the shrimp: In a medium bowl, whisk together oil, garlic, and red pepper flakes. Add shrimp and scallions and toss to coat; refrigerate for 30 minutes.

For the salad: In a small bowl, whisk together lime juice, oil, jalapeños, black pepper, and ⅛ teaspoon salt; let stand at room temperature while shrimp is marinating. In a large bowl, combine greens, papaya, avocado, and bell pepper.

Generously coat a grill or grill pan with cooking spray and heat to medium–high. Alternately thread shrimp and scallions onto 4 skewers. Lightly sprinkle shrimp and scallions with salt and grill, turning once and basting with any remaining marinade, until shrimp just turn pink, 2 to 3 minutes per side. Remove shrimp and scallions from skewers and add to salad mixture. Add dressing and toss gently. Arrange salad on 4 plates and serve.

Makes 4 (generous 2-cup) servings

NUTRITION AT A GLANCE

Per serving with papaya: 369 calories, 21.5 g fat, 3 g saturated fat, 26 g protein, 19 g carbohydrate, 7 g fiber, 265 mg sodium

Per serving without papaya: 339 calories, 21.5 g fat, 3 g saturated fat, 26 g protein, 12 g carbohydrate, 6 g fiber, 262 mg sodium

Provençal Bouillabaisse

PREP TIME: 25 minutes   COOK TIME: 25 minutes

This delicious shellfish stew is said to have originated in the sunny port city of Marseille in the south of France. Add a little fresh or dried chile if you like a subtle kick of heat.

- 1 tablespoon extra-virgin olive oil
- 1 small fennel bulb, finely chopped, fronds finely chopped for garnish
- 1 small leek, white part only, finely chopped
- 2 garlic cloves, smashed and peeled
- ¼ teaspoon dried thyme
- ¼ cup white wine
- 2 large plum tomatoes, chopped
- 3 cups lower-sodium chicken broth
-    Pinch saffron
- 1 pound cod or haddock fillets, skin removed, fish cut into 2-inch pieces
- ½ pound mussels (about 8), cleaned
- ½ pound littleneck clams or cockles (about 8), scrubbed

In a large nonstick saucepan, heat oil over medium heat. Add fennel bulb, leek, garlic, and thyme; cover, reduce heat to medium-low, and cook until vegetables are softened, about 5 minutes. Stir in wine and tomatoes; cook, uncovered, until liquid has almost evaporated, about 1 minute.

Add broth and saffron; bring to a simmer. Add cod, cover, and cook for 5 minutes. Add mussels and clams, cover, and cook until shells are opened, about 5 minutes more. Discard any shellfish that haven't opened. Ladle bouillabaisse into 4 large bowls, sprinkle with chopped fennel fronds, and serve hot.

Makes 4 (2-cup) servings

NUTRITION AT A GLANCE
Per serving: 210 calories, 5 g fat, 1 g saturated fat, 28 g protein, 10 g carbohydrate, 2 g fiber, 560 mg sodium

EASY SUMMER POULTRY

Versatile, tasty, and easy to prepare, chicken and turkey breast make perfect summer foods (try to buy antibiotic- and hormone-free brands and avoid fatty duck). Whether you're grinding poultry for flavorful burgers; cubing, skewering, and grilling it; chopping it into salads; or slicing it into cutlets for poaching or pan-searing, there's a poultry cooking method (or two!) for any summer day or night.

The dishes you'll find in this chapter take their cues from all over the globe. There are Asian-flavored turkey meatballs tucked into cooling lettuce leaves, a Mediterranean-style chicken burger, and pan-seared chicken breasts served with a tangy Mexican-inspired tomatillo salsa.

Pantry basics (like curry powder, cayenne, and other dried spices and herbs, extra-virgin olive oil, Dijon mustard, canned beans, and low-sodium soy sauce) will make fast work of dishes like Curried Chicken Salad with Peanuts, Spicy Chicken and Black Bean Tacos, and Quick Chicken Tagine. Since poultry is a family favorite, you're sure to please no matter which dish you choose.

◄ *Grilled Chicken with Savory Asian Plum Sauce (page 128)*

Grilled Chicken with Savory Asian Plum Sauce

PREP TIME: 15 minutes   **MARINATING TIME:** 15 minutes   **COOK TIME:** 30 minutes

Combined with sesame oil, fresh ginger, and mirin (Japanese rice wine), fresh plums make a savory sauce for simple grilled chicken.

- 4 (6-ounce) boneless, skinless chicken breasts
- 1 tablespoon fresh lime juice
- 3 garlic cloves, minced
- 2 teaspoons extra-virgin olive oil
- 1 teaspoon toasted sesame oil
- 6 medium plums, cut into eighths
- 2 tablespoons mirin
- 2 teaspoons finely grated lime zest
- 1 teaspoon grated fresh ginger
- ¼ teaspoon salt
  Freshly ground black pepper
  Fresh herbs, greens, or sprouts for garnish

In a resealable plastic bag, combine chicken, lime juice, garlic, and olive oil; turn to coat. Marinate chicken at room temperature for 15 minutes or refrigerate overnight.

In a medium nonstick skillet, heat sesame oil over medium heat. Add plums, mirin, lime zest, ginger, salt, and pepper to taste. Cook, stirring gently, until plums are softened, 10 to 15 minutes, depending on ripeness (do not allow plums to completely lose their shape). Remove the pan from the heat, cover, and keep warm.

Lightly coat a grill or grill pan with cooking spray and heat to medium-high. Remove chicken from marinade and grill until cooked through, 5 to 7 minutes per side. Discard any remaining marinade. Divide chicken among 4 plates and serve warm, topped with plum sauce. Garnish as desired.

Makes 4 servings

NUTRITION AT A GLANCE
Per serving: 285 calories, 6 g fat, 1 g saturated fat, 40 g protein, 15 g carbohydrate, 2 g fiber, 260 mg sodium

Garlicky Chicken Skewers

PREP TIME: 15 minutes   **COOK TIME:** 10 minutes

Grilled with garden-fresh eggplant and zucchini, these easy, delicious chicken skewers are perfect for an outdoor grill-fest on a hot summer night.

1½ pounds boneless, skinless chicken breasts, cut into 1-inch pieces

3 garlic cloves, finely minced

2 teaspoons dried rosemary

3 teaspoons extra-virgin olive oil

Salt

Freshly ground black pepper

1 small eggplant (1 pound), peeled and cut into ½-inch cubes

3 small zucchini, cut into ½-inch-thick rounds

Special equipment

8 (12-inch) skewers

Lightly coat a grill or grill pan with cooking spray and heat to medium-high.

In a medium bowl, combine chicken, garlic, rosemary, 2 teaspoons of the oil, ¼ teaspoon salt, and ⅛ teaspoon pepper; stir to coat well. Thread equal amounts of chicken onto 4 skewers.

In the same bowl, toss eggplant and zucchini pieces with remaining 1 teaspoon oil. Thread eggplant and zucchini pieces evenly onto 4 remaining skewers. Lightly season with salt and pepper.

Grill chicken and vegetable skewers, turning every 2 minutes, until chicken is cooked through and vegetables are tender and lightly browned, about 8 minutes for chicken and 10 minutes for vegetables. Serve warm.

Makes 4 (2-skewer) servings

NUTRITION AT A GLANCE
Per serving: 260 calories, 6 g fat, 1 g saturated fat, 42 g protein, 11 g carbohydrate, 5 g fiber, 270 mg sodium

PHASE 2

PHASE 1
(without bun)

Pulled Turkey Sandwiches

PREP TIME: 5 minutes   **COOK TIME:** 50 minutes

Long popular in the American South and favorite summertime fare, pulled meats are cooked slowly until they are tender enough to be easily pulled apart or sliced. Our version, made with turkey breast rather than traditional pork or beef, has a deliciously sweet and tangy sauce. Turkey breast is inexpensive and easy to find, but you can also use turkey tenderloins, if you like. Serve the sandwiches with Citrusy Hot Pepper Slaw (page 93) if you are on Phase 2.

1 (14-ounce) can lower-sodium chicken broth	1 tablespoon Worcestershire sauce
1 (8-ounce) can no-salt-added tomato sauce	2 teaspoons mustard powder
2 tablespoons apple cider vinegar	1 teaspoon red pepper flakes
2 tablespoons sugar-free pancake syrup	1½ pounds boneless, skinless turkey breast, cut into 4 or 5 pieces
3 garlic cloves, minced	4 whole-wheat or whole-grain hamburger buns (optional)

In a medium saucepan, combine broth, tomato sauce, vinegar, syrup, garlic, Worcestershire sauce, mustard, and pepper flakes; bring to a boil over medium-high heat. Reduce the heat to low and add turkey; cover and simmer for 30 minutes.

Using a slotted spoon, transfer turkey to a large bowl to cool for about 10 minutes. Continue cooking sauce, uncovered, until reduced by half, 10 to 15 minutes (you should have at least 1 cup). Remove from the heat and transfer ½ cup of the sauce to a small bowl, leaving remaining sauce in the pan.

Using 2 forks, shred (pull) turkey. Return pulled turkey to the saucepan and stir to coat evenly with remaining sauce. Cook over low heat just to warm through, about 3 minutes. Divide turkey meat among buns, if using, and drizzle evenly with reserved sauce. Serve warm.

Makes 4 servings

NUTRITION AT A GLANCE
Per serving with bun: 350 calories, 4 g fat, 0.5 g saturated fat, 48 g protein, 30 g carbohydrate, 4 g fiber, 590 mg sodium
Per serving without bun: 230 calories, 2 g fat, 0 g saturated fat, 45 g protein, 8 g carbohydrate, 1 g fiber, 380 mg sodium

Mediterranean Chicken Burgers

PREP TIME: 15 minutes   **COOK TIME:** 10 minutes

Artichoke hearts and sun-dried tomatoes combined with a little chopped garlic and a handful of aromatic basil leaves make this juicy chicken burger one of our favorite hot-weather dishes. The burgers are great pan-grilled but can also be grilled outdoors.

1   (13¾-ounce) can quartered artichoke hearts in water, drained

¼   cup sun-dried tomatoes in oil (about 6), cut into thin strips

1   pound ground chicken breast

1   large egg yolk

1   tablespoon Dijon mustard

2   teaspoons Worcestershire sauce

1   garlic clove, minced

2   tablespoons chopped fresh basil, plus 12 whole basil leaves

4   whole-wheat or whole-grain hamburger buns, lightly toasted (optional)

In a small bowl, combine artichoke hearts and tomatoes.

In a large bowl, stir together chicken, egg yolk, mustard, Worcestershire sauce, garlic, and chopped basil. Form mixture into 4 patties, about ½ inch thick.

Lightly coat a large nonstick skillet with cooking spray and heat over medium-high heat. Add burgers and cook until cooked through, about 5 minutes per side.

Place basil leaves on buns, if using, and top with burgers. Top each burger with artichoke mixture and serve.

Makes 4 servings

NUTRITION AT A GLANCE
Per serving with bun: 340 calories, 8 g fat, 1.5 g saturated fat, 34 g protein, 36 g carbohydrate, 7 g fiber, 830 mg sodium
Per serving without bun: 230 calories, 6 g fat, 1 g saturated fat, 31 g protein, 14 g carbohydrate, 4 g fiber, 620 mg sodium

Jalapeño Turkey Burgers

PREP TIME: 10 minutes   COOK TIME: 12 minutes

If you're a real fan of heat, use extra jalapeños (or any other variety of spicy fresh pepper) for these tasty burgers. You can also try substituting ground chicken breast or lean ground pork for the turkey.

1   pound ground turkey breast

1   large egg yolk

1   small jalapeño, seeded and chopped

3   garlic cloves, minced

2   teaspoons Worcestershire sauce

2   tablespoons tomato paste

2   ounces shredded reduced-fat Monterey Jack cheese (½ cup)

4   whole-wheat or whole-grain hamburger buns, lightly toasted (optional)

In a large bowl, stir together turkey, egg yolk, jalapeño, garlic, Worcestershire sauce, and tomato paste. Form mixture into 4 patties, about ¾ inch thick.

Lightly coat a large nonstick skillet with cooking spray and heat over medium–high heat. Add burgers and cook until cooked through, about 5 minutes per side. Top each burger with cheese and cook until cheese melts, about 1 minute more. Serve on buns, if using.

Makes 4 servings

NUTRITION AT A GLANCE

Per serving with bun: 301 calories, 8 g fat, 2.5 g saturated fat, 36 g protein, 26 g carbohydrate, 4 g fiber, 500 mg sodium

Per serving without bun: 187 calories, 6 g fat, 2 g saturated fat, 32 g protein, 4 g carbohydrate, 0 g fiber, 290 mg sodium

Quick Chicken Tagine

PREP TIME: 25 minutes   **COOK TIME: 25 minutes**

Tagine is a Moroccan stew made with meat or poultry, vegetables, olives, and preserved lemon, which can be found in specialty stores and thinly sliced as a garnish, if desired.

2 garlic cloves

2 (3-inch) pieces lemon zest

3 tablespoons chopped fresh parsley, plus leaves for garnish

½ teaspoon ground coriander

½ teaspoon ground cumin

¼ teaspoon ground cinnamon

   Freshly ground black pepper

1 tablespoon extra-virgin olive oil

1½ pounds boneless, skinless chicken breasts, cut into 1-inch cubes

1 medium onion, chopped

1 (14-ounce) can no-salt-added diced tomatoes, with juices

3 tablespoons fresh lemon juice

2 medium zucchini, cut into ½-inch cubes

20 pitted medium green olives, halved

   Pinch salt

On a cutting board, finely chop 1 clove of the garlic together with 1 piece of the lemon zest and 1 tablespoon of the parsley to make a rough paste; transfer to a small bowl and set aside. Mince remaining garlic clove and place in another small bowl; mix in coriander, cumin, cinnamon, and pepper.

In a large nonstick skillet, heat oil over medium–high heat. Add chicken and cook, turning occasionally, until lightly browned, 3 to 4 minutes. Transfer chicken to a plate.

Reduce the heat under the skillet to medium and add onion and spice mixture; cook, stirring constantly, until onion is softened and spices are aromatic, 2 to 3 minutes. Add tomatoes and their juices and lemon juice, scraping up any brown bits clinging to the skillet; bring to a simmer. Return chicken pieces and their juices to the skillet and cook for 5 minutes. Add zucchini, olives, remaining lemon zest, and remaining 2 tablespoons parsley; stir gently to combine. Reduce the heat to low, cover, and cook until chicken is cooked through, 10 minutes more. Lightly season with salt and pepper. Divide tagine among 4 bowls, top with reserved parsley paste, and garnish with parsley leaves.

Makes 4 (1½-cup) servings

NUTRITION AT A GLANCE

Per serving: 310 calories, 10 g fat, 1 g saturated fat, 42 g protein, 13 g carbohydrate, 4 g fiber, 380 mg sodium

Curried Chicken Salad with Peanuts

PREP TIME: 15 minutes   **COOK TIME:** 15 minutes

Sliced snow peas, chopped scallions, and crunchy roasted peanuts put a South Beach Diet twist on popular curried chicken salad.

2   teaspoons extra-virgin olive oil

1½ pounds boneless, skinless chicken breasts

2   tablespoons fresh lemon juice

12 ounces snow peas, trimmed and cut into ½-inch pieces

½   cup nonfat or low-fat plain yogurt

¼   cup mayonnaise

1   tablespoon curry powder

2   teaspoons Dijon mustard

1   teaspoon finely grated lemon zest

¼   teaspoon salt

2   celery stalks, finely chopped

1   small bunch scallions, chopped

    Freshly ground black pepper

⅓   cup unsalted roasted peanuts, chopped

In a large nonstick skillet, heat oil over medium–high heat. Add chicken and 1 tablespoon of the lemon juice; cook until chicken is cooked through, 5 to 6 minutes per side. Transfer chicken to a cutting board and let cool to room temperature. When cool, cut into ½-inch cubes.

While chicken is cooking, bring a medium saucepan of lightly salted water to a boil. Add snow peas and cook for 1 minute. Drain snow peas in a colander and immediately run under very cold water for 1 minute to stop cooking. Drain again and pat dry.

In a large bowl, whisk together yogurt, mayonnaise, curry powder, mustard, lemon zest, salt, and remaining 1 tablespoon lemon juice. Add chicken, snow peas, celery, and scallions to yogurt mixture and toss to combine; season with pepper to taste. Divide chicken salad among 4 plates, sprinkle with peanuts, and serve.

Makes 4 (1½-cup) servings

NUTRITION AT A GLANCE
Per serving: 440 calories, 22 g fat, 3.5 g saturated fat, 47 g protein, 15 g carbohydrate, 4 g fiber, 410 mg sodium

Spicy Chicken and Black Bean Tacos

PREP TIME: 15 minutes **COOK TIME:** 15 minutes

Seasoned with a flavorful dry rub that's put together with simple pantry basics, these soft tacos are tasty and easy to prepare. For other dry rub ideas, see page 11.

Rub

- 2 teaspoons garlic powder
- 2 teaspoons paprika
- 2 teaspoons dried thyme
- 1 teaspoon cayenne
- 1 teaspoon freshly ground black pepper

Chicken

- 1 pound boneless, skinless chicken breasts

- 1½ tablespoons extra-virgin olive oil
- 1 medium onion, chopped
- 1 (15-ounce) can black beans, rinsed and drained
- 1 medium tomato, chopped
- ¼ cup minced fresh cilantro, plus whole leaves for garnish
- 4 (8-inch) whole-wheat tortillas

For the rub: In a small bowl, combine garlic powder, paprika, thyme, cayenne, and black pepper.

For the chicken: Lightly pound each chicken breast to an even ½-inch thickness. Rub a thick layer of the spice mixture onto both sides of each chicken breast.

In a large heavy skillet, heat 1 tablespoon of the oil over high heat until hot but not smoking. Add chicken and cook until blackened on both sides and cooked through, 2 to 3 minutes per side. Transfer chicken to a cutting board.

Reduce heat to medium and add remaining ½ tablespoon oil and onion to the skillet. Cook, stirring to scrape up any brown bits clinging to the bottom of the skillet, until onion is softened, 1 to 2 minutes. Add beans and cook until heated through, 2 to 3 minutes. Remove from the heat and stir in tomato and minced cilantro.

Warm tortillas according to package directions. Cut chicken on the diagonal into ½-inch-thick slices. Place tortillas on 4 plates. Divide chicken and beans among tortillas. Fold tortillas into cones and top with cilantro leaves.

Makes 4 servings

NUTRITION AT A GLANCE

Per serving: 410 calories, 10 g fat, 1 g saturated fat, 36 g protein, 42 g carbohydrate, 8 g fiber, 540 mg sodium

Asian Turkey Meatballs in Lettuce Cups

PREP TIME: 20 minutes   COOK TIME: 15 minutes

Spicy fresh ginger, dark nutty sesame oil, and sweet rice vinegar add an Asian flair to this flavorful dish. Add more lettuce, if desired, so that guests can make roll-ups with single meatballs.

Dressing

- 1 tablespoon Asian fish sauce
- 1 tablespoon rice vinegar
- ½ teaspoon toasted sesame oil
- Pinch red pepper flakes

Meatballs

- 1 pound ground turkey breast
- 2 garlic cloves, minced
- 1 tablespoon grated fresh ginger
- 1 tablespoon toasted sesame oil
- 2 teaspoons rice vinegar
- 2 teaspoons low-sodium soy sauce
- 12 large Boston lettuce leaves
- 1 small cucumber, cut into matchsticks
- 1 cup mint leaves

For the dressing: In a small bowl, whisk together fish sauce, vinegar, sesame oil, and pepper flakes; set aside at room temperature.

For the meatballs: In a large bowl, stir together turkey, garlic, ginger, sesame oil, vinegar, and soy sauce. Form mixture into 24 (2-inch) meatballs.

Lightly coat a large nonstick skillet with cooking spray and heat to medium–high. Add meatballs in two batches and cook, turning occasionally, until browned on all sides, 5 to 7 minutes for each batch.

Lay 3 lettuce leaves on each of 4 plates. Place 2 meatballs on top of each leaf. Top meatballs with cucumber and mint leaves, drizzle with dressing, and serve.

Makes 4 (6-meatball) servings

NUTRITION AT A GLANCE
Per serving: 180 calories, 6 g fat, 0.5 g saturated fat, 30 g protein, 4 g carbohydrate, 0 g fiber, 480 mg sodium

Pan-Seared Chicken with Roasted Tomatillo Salsa

PREP TIME: 15 minutes   **COOK TIME:** 30 minutes

Tangy and delicious, fresh tomatillos are found in Latin American groceries and some supermarkets. The canned version can be substituted if fresh are not available.

12 ounces fresh tomatillos	1 small jalapeño, seeded and minced
3 teaspoons extra-virgin olive oil	1 tablespoon fresh lime juice
1 medium onion, chopped	4 (6-ounce) boneless, skinless chicken breasts
2 garlic cloves, chopped	Salt and freshly ground black pepper
½ cup cilantro leaves	

Remove and discard papery skin from tomatillos; rinse and pat dry.

Heat the broiler. Place tomatillos on a foil-lined broiler pan; broil for 8 to 10 minutes, turning halfway through, until softened and blackened on all sides. Transfer tomatillos and their juices to a blender or food processor.

In a medium nonstick skillet, heat 2 teaspoons of the oil over medium heat. Add onion and garlic; cook, stirring occasionally, until softened and lightly browned, about 5 minutes. Transfer to the blender or food processor with the tomatillos and add cilantro, jalapeño, and lime juice. Pulse for 1 minute, until ingredients form a rough purée.

Lightly pound each chicken breast to an even ½-inch thickness; season lightly with salt and black pepper.

In a large heavy skillet, heat remaining 1 teaspoon oil over high heat until hot but not smoking. Add chicken breasts, reduce the heat to medium-high, and cook until lightly browned and cooked through, 4 to 5 minutes per side. Transfer chicken to a cutting board.

Transfer tomatillo salsa to the hot skillet and cook over medium-high heat, stirring constantly, for about 1 minute, until salsa has a darker, thicker color and texture. Remove from the heat.

Slice chicken breasts on the diagonal into ½-inch-thick slices. Place ¼ cup of the salsa on each of 4 plates, arrange chicken slices on top, and top with additional salsa. Serve warm.

Makes 4 servings

NUTRITION AT A GLANCE
Per serving: 260 calories, 7 g fat, 1 g saturated fat, 41 g protein, 9 g carbohydrate, 2 g fiber, 115 mg sodium

Turkey Cutlets with Vegetable Couscous

PREP TIME: 20 minutes   **MARINATING TIME:** 15 minutes   **COOK TIME:** 8 minutes

Warm couscous tossed with crisp cucumber, yellow bell pepper, sweet tomatoes, olive oil, and a touch of red wine vinegar makes a perfect side for marinated turkey cutlets. The couscous is also good with a simple piece of grilled chicken or fish.

1½ pounds turkey cutlets

3 garlic cloves, minced

3 tablespoons chopped fresh parsley

1 tablespoon plus 2 teaspoons extra-virgin olive oil

2 teaspoons finely grated lemon zest

⅛ teaspoon red pepper flakes

1 small yellow bell pepper, finely chopped

1 cup cherry tomatoes, halved

1 small cucumber, peeled and cut into ¼-inch cubes

1 tablespoon minced red onion

1 tablespoon red wine vinegar

¼ teaspoon salt

½ cup whole-wheat couscous

In a resealable plastic bag, combine turkey, garlic, parsley, 1 tablespoon of the oil, lemon zest, and pepper flakes; turn to coat well. Marinate at room temperature for 15 minutes or refrigerate overnight.

While turkey is marinating, in a large bowl combine remaining 2 teaspoons oil, bell pepper, tomatoes, cucumber, onion, vinegar, and salt.

Prepare couscous according to package directions. Add hot couscous to vegetable mixture and stir well; keep warm.

Lightly coat a nonstick skillet with cooking spray and heat over medium-high heat. Add turkey and marinade to the skillet and cook until cooked through, about 2 minutes per side. Serve warm with vegetable couscous.

Makes 4 servings

NUTRITION AT A GLANCE
Per serving: 310 calories, 7 g fat, 1 g saturated fat, 45 g protein, 16 g carbohydrate, 3 g fiber, 300 mg sodium

Grilled Chicken Fajitas

PREP TIME: 15 minutes   **MARINATING TIME:** 20 minutes   **COOK TIME:** 25 minutes

Fresh lime-and-garlic-marinated grilled chicken paired with charred bell peppers and sweet red onion makes a tasty filling for these delicious fajitas. Top with a dollop of salsa and nonfat or low-fat plain yogurt, if you like.

1½ pounds boneless, skinless chicken breasts	1 large red bell pepper, quartered
2 tablespoons fresh lime juice	1 large green bell pepper, quartered
3 garlic cloves, minced	1 large red onion, cut into ½-inch-thick rounds
½ small jalapeño, seeded and minced	2 teaspoons extra-virgin olive oil
Salt and freshly ground black pepper	4 (8-inch) whole-wheat tortillas

In a resealable plastic bag, combine chicken, lime juice, garlic, and jalapeño; turn to coat well. Marinate chicken at room temperature for 20 minutes or refrigerate overnight. Remove chicken from marinade and season lightly with salt and black pepper.

Lightly coat a grill or grill pan with cooking spray and heat to medium-high. Grill chicken until cooked through, about 5 minutes per side. Transfer to a cutting board.

While chicken is cooking, in a medium bowl toss bell peppers and onion with oil. Using a grill basket or grill topper, if necessary, grill vegetables, turning occasionally, until softened and lightly charred, 15 to 20 minutes. Transfer onions to a platter. Transfer peppers to a cutting board and cut into thin strips; transfer to the platter with onions.

Grill tortillas until warm and lightly browned, about 30 seconds per side. Wrap in foil to keep warm.

Slice chicken breasts into ½-inch-thick pieces. Place on the platter with vegetables and serve with warmed tortillas.

Makes 4 servings

NUTRITION AT A GLANCE
Per serving: 350 calories, 7 g fat, 1 g saturated fat, 43 g protein, 28 g carbohydrate, 5 g fiber, 340 mg sodium

Jerk Chicken with Cool Romaine Salad

PREP TIME: 20 minutes   **MARINATING TIME:** 1 hour   **COOK TIME:** 12 minutes

Traditional Jamaican "jerk" is a blend of herbs and spices that often includes chiles, thyme, cinnamon, ginger, cloves, and garlic. It is typically rubbed onto meats before cooking. Look for jerk seasoning in the spice section of most supermarkets or make your own if you have time (see recipe on page 11). The chicken can also be grilled outdoors.

1½	pounds boneless, skinless chicken breasts
1	tablespoon jerk seasoning
2	tablespoons reduced-fat sour cream
1	tablespoon fresh lime juice
1	(1-pound) head romaine lettuce, chopped (8 cups)
1	large cucumber, peeled and sliced
2	large plum tomatoes, chopped
2	scallions, chopped
¼	teaspoon salt

Pound chicken breasts to an even ½-inch thickness. Lightly rub jerk seasoning on both sides of chicken breasts. Refrigerate in an airtight container for at least 1 hour.

Lightly coat a large nonstick skillet with cooking spray and heat over medium-high heat. Add chicken and cook until cooked through, 4 to 5 minutes per side. Transfer to a cutting board, let rest for 5 minutes, then cut into ½-inch-thick slices.

While chicken is resting, in a large bowl combine sour cream and lime juice. Add lettuce, cucumber, tomatoes, scallions, and salt; toss well. Divide salad among 4 plates, top with chicken slices, and serve.

Makes 4 servings

NUTRITION AT A GLANCE
Per serving: 230 calories, 3.5 g fat, 1 g saturated fat, 42 g protein, 8 g carbohydrate, 3 g fiber, 480 mg sodium

Easy Summer Chicken Chili

PREP TIME: 20 minutes   **COOK TIME:** 25 minutes

Seasonal garden-fresh vegetables are combined with chunks of tender chicken and high-fiber beans in this light Phase 1 chili. Quick to prepare and perfect for cooler summer evenings, the recipe is easily doubled or tripled for a crowd.

- 1 small avocado, finely chopped
- 1 tablespoon fresh lime juice
- ¼ teaspoon salt
- 1 tablespoon extra-virgin olive oil
- 1 medium onion, chopped
- 1 small green bell pepper, chopped
- 1 small zucchini, thinly sliced
- 1 medium jalapeño, seeded and minced
- 1 teaspoon chili powder
- ½ teaspoon ground cumin
- 2 cups lower-sodium chicken broth
- 1 (15-ounce) can white beans, rinsed and drained
- 1 (14.5-ounce) can no-salt-added diced tomatoes, with juices
- 1 pound boneless, skinless chicken breasts, cut into 1-inch cubes

In a small bowl, gently stir together avocado, lime juice, and ⅛ teaspoon of the salt.

In a large saucepan, heat oil over medium–high heat. Add onion, bell pepper, zucchini, jalapeño, chili powder, and cumin; stir to coat. Cook, stirring occasionally, until vegetables have begun to soften, about 5 minutes. Stir in broth, beans, and tomatoes and their juices; bring to a simmer and cook for 10 minutes. Add chicken and remaining ⅛ teaspoon salt. Return to a simmer and cook until chicken is cooked through, 5 to 7 minutes. Divide chili among 4 bowls, top with avocado, and serve.

Makes 4 (2-cup) servings

NUTRITION AT A GLANCE
Per serving: 380 calories, 12 g fat, 2 g saturated fat, 36 g protein, 33 g carbohydrate, 10 g fiber, 560 mg sodium

BURGERS, DOGS, AND OTHER MEAT DISHES

Summer wouldn't be complete without hamburgers, hot dogs, and other delicious meat dishes. We stick with lean meat choices like reduced-fat beef hot dogs, sirloin steak, pork loin, lean ground beef, and leg of lamb to ensure the nutritional benefits and avoid the saturated fat. Where beef is concerned, ideally use grass-fed varieties or substitute superlean bison or beefalo (a cross between bison and domestic cattle). Since these meats are even leaner than regular lean beef, they need less cooking time for the tastiest results.

There's something original here for every meat lover. Take your pick of Feta-Stuffed Sirloin Burgers with Sun-Dried Tomato Mayonnaise or Chimichurri Burgers. Stir up your own tomato-pickle relish for hot dogs, or top them with a thick chipotle chili; spoon a fruity peach-lime salsa over thick pieces of pork tenderloin; and enjoy Middle Eastern meatballs. A summer filled with great options awaits you.

◀ *Chimichurri Burgers (page 148)*

Chimichurri Burgers

PREP TIME: 15 minutes   **COOK TIME:** 15 minutes

Made with loads of fresh parsley, onion, and garlic, chimichurri sauce is an Argentinean favorite for topping grilled meats. Our version adds red pepper flakes, which give these lightly seasoned burgers a bit of heat.

Sauce

1   cup parsley leaves

3   scallions, chopped

2   garlic cloves, chopped

2   tablespoons red wine vinegar

2   tablespoons water

1   tablespoon extra-virgin olive oil

½   teaspoon red pepper flakes

⅛   teaspoon salt

Burgers

1½   pounds extra-lean ground beef

2   teaspoons dried basil

¼   teaspoon freshly ground black pepper

⅛   teaspoon salt

4   whole-wheat or whole-grain hamburger buns, lightly toasted (optional)

For the sauce: In a blender or food processor, combine parsley, scallions, garlic, vinegar, water, oil, pepper flakes, and salt; pulse until just puréed, about 1 minute.

For the burgers: In a large bowl, combine beef, basil, black pepper, and salt. Form into 4 patties, about 1 inch thick.

Lightly coat a grill or grill pan with cooking spray and heat to medium-high. Grill burgers 5 to 6 minutes per side, or until a thermometer inserted into the thickest part registers 160°F. Serve burgers on buns, if using, topped with chimichurri sauce.

Makes 4 servings

NUTRITION AT A GLANCE

Per serving with bun: 450 calories, 21 g fat, 7 g saturated fat, 40 g protein, 25 g carbohydrate, 4 g fiber, 490 mg sodium

Per serving without bun: 330 calories, 19 g fat, 7 g saturated fat, 36 g protein, 3 g carbohydrate, 1 g fiber, 280 mg sodium

Beef Satay with Peanut Sauce

PREP TIME: 15 minutes   MARINATING TIME: 20 minutes   COOK TIME: 15 minutes

Rich and creamy, with just the right touch of spice, our peanut sauce is great for perking up tender grilled slices of top round beef. Don't worry if the slices are of different lengths when you cut them; if you thread the meat on the skewers lengthwise, through the ends and middle of each piece, the meat will cook uniformly on the grill.

Satay

- 3 garlic cloves, minced
- 2 tablespoons fresh lime juice
- 1 tablespoon grated fresh ginger
- ½ teaspoon toasted sesame oil
- 1½ pounds top round beef, trimmed and cut into ¾-inch-thick slices

Sauce

- ¼ cup creamy trans-fat-free peanut butter
- ¼ cup water
- 2 tablespoons low-sodium soy sauce
- 1 tablespoon plus 1½ teaspoons rice vinegar
- 2 garlic cloves, minced
- ⅛ teaspoon red pepper flakes

Special equipment

- 4 (12-inch) skewers

For the satay: In a 9- by 13-inch glass baking dish, combine garlic, lime juice, ginger, and sesame oil. Add beef and turn to coat with marinade. Cover the dish with plastic wrap and marinate beef at room temperature for 20 minutes.

For the sauce: In a medium bowl, whisk together peanut butter, water, soy sauce, vinegar, garlic, and pepper flakes.

Lightly coat a grill or grill pan with cooking spray and heat to medium-high. Thread equal amounts of sliced meat onto 4 skewers. Grill meat 5 to 7 minutes per side for medium-rare. Serve warm with peanut sauce drizzled evenly over the meat or on the side for dipping.

Makes 4 servings

NUTRITION AT A GLANCE
Per serving: 360 calories, 17 g fat, 4 g saturated fat, 43 g protein, 6 g carbohydrate, 1 g fiber, 460 mg sodium

Grilled Pork Tenderloin with Peach-Lime Salsa

PREP TIME: 15 minutes   **MARINATING TIME:** 10 minutes
COOK TIME: 30 minutes   **STAND TIME:** 10 minutes

Sweet and tangy peach-lime salsa, flavored with minced red onion and garden-fresh mint, brings beautiful color and exceptional taste to this simple grilled pork dish. Serve the tenderloin with Crisp Jícama Salad with Creamy Cilantro Dressing (page 70).

  2 garlic cloves, minced

  2 teaspoons extra-virgin olive oil

  ¼ teaspoon freshly ground black pepper

  1½ pounds pork tenderloin

  2 large peaches, peeled and cut into ½-inch pieces

  1 small red onion, minced

  ¼ cup finely chopped fresh mint

  3 tablespoons fresh lime juice

  ¼ teaspoon salt

In a small bowl, combine garlic, oil, and pepper to form a rough paste. Place pork in a 9- by 13-inch glass baking dish and coat with garlic paste; let stand at room temperature for 10 minutes.

While pork is standing, in another small bowl combine peaches, onion, mint, lime juice, and salt.

Lightly coat a grill or grill pan with cooking spray and heat to medium-high. Grill pork 12 to 14 minutes per side, or until a thermometer inserted into the thickest part reads 150°F to 155°F. Transfer pork to a cutting board and let rest for 5 to 10 minutes.

Slice pork into ½-inch-thick slices and serve warm with peach-lime salsa.

Makes 4 servings

NUTRITION AT A GLANCE
Per serving with salsa: 270 calories, 8 g fat, 2.5 g saturated fat, 37 g protein, 12 g carbohydrate, 2 g fiber, 230 mg sodium
Per serving without salsa: 228 calories, 8 g fat, 2.5 g saturated fat, 36 g protein, 1 g carbohydrate, 0 g fiber, 85 mg sodium

Chipotle Chili Dogs

PREP TIME: 15 minutes   COOK TIME: 20 minutes

This delicious grilled chili dog gets its extra-special smoky flavor from canned chipotle chiles, which can be found in the Latin American section of most large supermarkets. See page 253 for more on chipotles.

1 teaspoon extra-virgin olive oil

1 small onion, finely chopped

2 garlic cloves, minced

½ pound extra-lean ground beef

2 tablespoons tomato paste

1 canned chipotle chile in adobo, chopped, plus 1 teaspoon sauce from can

¾ cup lower-sodium beef broth

4 reduced-fat beef hot dogs

4 whole-wheat or whole-grain hot dog buns, lightly toasted (optional)

In a medium saucepan, heat oil over medium heat. Add onion and garlic; cook, stirring occasionally, until translucent, 4 to 5 minutes. Add beef, increase the heat to high, and cook, breaking up meat with a spoon and stirring just until all pink is gone, 2 to 3 minutes more. Reduce the heat to medium and stir in tomato paste, chile, and adobo sauce. Add broth and bring to a simmer. Reduce the heat to low, cover, and cook until meat is cooked through, about 5 minutes.

While chili is cooking, lightly coat a grill or grill pan with cooking spray and heat to medium-high. Grill hot dogs, turning occasionally, until lightly browned and heated through, 5 to 7 minutes. Serve hot dogs on buns, if using, topped with chili.

Makes 4 servings

NUTRITION AT A GLANCE
Per serving with bun: 340 calories, 15 g fat, 6 g saturated fat, 23 g protein, 29 g carbohydrate, 4 g fiber, 920 mg sodium
Per serving without bun: 220 calories, 12 g fat, 5 g saturated fat, 19 g protein, 7 g carbohydrate, 0 g fiber, 720 mg sodium

Herb-Marinated Sirloin with Roasted Asparagus and Tomatoes

PREP TIME: 10 minutes   MARINATING TIME: 30 minutes   COOK TIME: 30 minutes

Drizzled with extra-virgin olive oil and sprinkled with salt, roasted asparagus spears and tiny tomatoes emerge from the oven golden and sweet. Although especially good with steak, the vegetables can also be served with chicken or fish—or as a vegetarian side—all season long. We pan-grill the steak here, but it can also be grilled outdoors.

½	teaspoon garlic powder
½	teaspoon dried marjoram
½	teaspoon dried thyme
½	teaspoon freshly ground black pepper
¼	teaspoon salt
1	(1¾-pound) sirloin steak, about 1½ inches thick
1	pound medium-thick asparagus, trimmed
1½	cups grape tomatoes
2	teaspoons extra-virgin olive oil

In a small bowl, combine garlic powder, marjoram, thyme, pepper, and ⅛ teaspoon of the salt. Rub onto steak. Place steak on a plate, cover with plastic wrap, and let steak sit at room temperature for 30 minutes.

Lightly coat a heavy skillet with cooking spray and heat over medium-high heat. Pan-grill steak 10 minutes per side for medium-rare. Transfer to a cutting board and let sit for 5 to 10 minutes.

While steak is resting, heat the oven to 450°F. Spread asparagus and tomatoes on a baking sheet, drizzle with oil, sprinkle with remaining ⅛ teaspoon salt, and toss to combine. Roast until tomatoes are bursting and asparagus is tender, 8 to 10 minutes.

While vegetables are roasting, thinly slice steak. Divide steak and vegetables among 4 plates and serve warm.

Makes 4 servings

NUTRITION AT A GLANCE
Per serving: 280 calories, 10 g fat, 3.5 g saturated fat, 40 g protein, 7 g carbohydrate, 3 g fiber, 250 mg sodium

Carne Asada

PREP TIME: 15 minutes **MARINATING TIME:** 20 minutes
COOK TIME: 25 minutes **STAND TIME:** 10 minutes

Carne asada means "grilled meat" in Spanish and is also the name of one of Mexico's most popular dishes. Purchase the fresh salsa from your supermarket. You can also try grilled scallions instead of red onion, if you like.

¼ cup fresh lime juice

2 garlic cloves, minced

½ teaspoon freshly ground black pepper

⅛ teaspoon salt

1 (1½-pound) flank steak, about 1 inch thick

1 large red onion, sliced into ¼-inch-thick rounds

½ teaspoon extra-virgin olive oil

1 small avocado, sliced into ¼-inch-thick pieces

1 cup fresh tomato salsa

In a 9- by 13-inch glass baking dish, combine lime juice, garlic, pepper, and salt. Add steak and turn to coat. Cover the dish with plastic wrap and marinate steak at room temperature for 20 minutes, turning once.

Lightly coat a grill or grill pan with cooking spray and heat to medium-high. Grill steak, basting with any remaining marinade, 5 to 7 minutes per side for medium-rare. Transfer to a cutting board and let rest for 5 to 10 minutes.

While steak is resting, in a medium bowl toss onion with oil. Grill, turning occasionally, until golden, 4 to 5 minutes. Cut steak into thin slices across the grain and divide among 4 plates. Serve with onion, avocado, and salsa.

Makes 4 servings

NUTRITION AT A GLANCE
Per serving: 360 calories, 17 g fat, 5 g saturated fat, 38 g protein, 13 g carbohydrate, 3 g fiber, 440 mg sodium

Kofta Skewers with Peppers

PREP TIME: 20 minutes   **COOK TIME:** 17 minutes

A deliciously spiced "meatball," kofta (the word means "pounded meat" in Persian) is enjoyed in many Middle Eastern and South Asian countries. Here the meat is formed into sausages and grilled on skewers for a fun presentation. If you're cooking outdoors, use a grill topper or vegetable basket to keep the peppers from falling through the grate.

1 pound extra-lean ground beef

½ pound lean ground lamb

1 small onion, grated

¼ cup chopped fresh parsley

2 tablespoons tomato paste

2 garlic cloves, minced

1 tablespoon ground cumin

1 teaspoon red pepper flakes

¼ teaspoon salt

2 medium bell peppers, any color, cut into ½-inch-wide strips

1 teaspoon extra-virgin olive oil

Special equipment

8 (12-inch) skewers

In a large bowl, combine beef, lamb, onion, parsley, tomato paste, garlic, cumin, pepper flakes, and salt. Divide meat mixture into 8 equal portions. Form each portion into a 6-inch sausage shape around a skewer.

In a medium bowl, toss peppers with oil.

Lightly coat a grill or grill pan with cooking spray and heat to medium-high. Grill meat, turning frequently, until browned on all sides and cooked through, about 15 minutes. Halfway through cooking, place peppers on the grill and cook, turning frequently, until lightly charred on all sides, 8 to 10 minutes. Serve kofta hot with peppers.

Makes 4 (2-skewer) servings

NUTRITION AT A GLANCE
Per serving: 360 calories, 21 g fat, 9 g saturated fat, 35 g protein, 8 g carbohydrate, 2 g fiber, 330 mg sodium

Pork Kebabs with Scallion-Chili Paste

PREP TIME: 15 minutes   COOK TIME: 15 minutes

Ground fresh chili paste, also sold as "garlic chili paste," is the secret ingredient that perks up this tender pork loin dish. Look for a brand without sugar in the Asian section of most large supermarkets. You can also try chili paste in burgers, stir-fries, homemade mayonnaise or other sauces—and even on scrambled eggs!

6 scallions, roughly chopped

½ cup cilantro leaves

1 tablespoon rice vinegar

2 teaspoons Asian fish sauce

1 teaspoon chili paste (from a jar)

1½ pounds pork top loin, cut into 1-inch cubes

2 medium zucchini, cut into 1-inch-thick rounds

2 garlic cloves, minced

1 teaspoon canola oil

Salt and freshly ground black pepper

Special equipment

8 (12-inch) skewers

In a food processor, combine scallions and cilantro; pulse until finely chopped. Add vinegar, fish sauce, and chili paste; process until a rough paste forms, about 30 seconds. Transfer scallion–chili paste to a medium bowl, add pork, and turn to coat well.

In another medium bowl, toss zucchini with garlic and oil. Thread pork and zucchini evenly onto skewers, alternating pieces.

Lightly coat a grill or grill pan with cooking spray and heat to medium-high. Grill kebabs, turning frequently, until pork is just cooked through, 10 to 12 minutes. Season lightly with salt and pepper and serve.

Makes 4 (2-skewer) servings

NUTRITION AT A GLANCE
Per serving: 240 calories, 5 g fat, 1.5 g saturated fat, 40 g protein, 6 g carbohydrate, 2 g fiber, 560 mg sodium

Hot Dogs with Homemade Tomato-Pickle Relish

PREP TIME: 15 minutes   COOK TIME: 10 minutes

Our colorful fresh pickle relish is healthier and more vibrant-tasting than most supermarket brands—and free from preservatives, sugar, and excess salt. It's good not only on hot dogs but on burgers and sandwiches as well.

¾ cup finely chopped bell pepper (mix of green and yellow)

1 medium plum tomato, finely chopped

¼ cup finely chopped red onion

2 tablespoons finely chopped dill pickle

1 tablespoon cider vinegar

¼ teaspoon granular sugar substitute

⅛ teaspoon salt

4 reduced-fat beef hot dogs

4 whole-wheat or whole-grain hot dog buns, lightly toasted (optional)

In a small bowl, combine pepper, tomato, onion, pickle, vinegar, sugar substitute, and salt.

Lightly coat a grill or grill pan with cooking spray and heat to medium-high. Grill hot dogs, turning occasionally, until lightly browned and heated through, 5 to 7 minutes. Serve hot dogs on buns, if using, topped with relish.

Makes 4 servings

NUTRITION AT A GLANCE
Per serving with bun: 230 calories, 9 g fat, 3.5 g saturated fat, 10 g protein, 28 g carbohydrate, 4 g fiber, 850 mg sodium
Per serving without bun: 110 calories, 7 g fat, 3 g saturated fat, 7 g protein, 6 g carbohydrate, 0 g fiber, 640 mg sodium

Pork Pinchos with Shredded Cabbage Salad

PREP TIME: 30 minutes   **MARINATING TIME:** 30 minutes   **COOK TIME:** 15 minutes

Traditional Spanish tapas fare, pork pinchos make a great main course when served with a salad of tender cabbage and creamy avocado sweetened with juicy orange sections. An extra squeeze of orange just before serving is a nice touch.

Pork

- 2 teaspoons paprika
- 1 teaspoon ground cumin
- ½ teaspoon garlic powder
- ¼ teaspoon cayenne
- 1½ pounds pork center loin, cut into 1-inch cubes

Salad

- 1 (1-pound) head Napa cabbage, thinly sliced (6 cups)
- 1 seedless orange, peeled and chopped
- 1 small avocado, finely chopped
- 2 scallions, thinly sliced
- 1 tablespoon extra-virgin olive oil
- ¼ teaspoon salt
- ¼ teaspoon freshly ground black pepper

  Pinch cayenne
- 1 small orange, peeled and cut into 8 wedges

Special equipment

- 4 (12-inch) skewers

For the pork: In a large bowl, combine paprika, cumin, garlic powder, and cayenne. Add pork and turn to coat; cover the bowl with plastic wrap and let sit at room temperature for 30 minutes. Thread pork evenly onto skewers.

For the salad: In another large bowl, combine cabbage, chopped orange, avocado, scallions, oil, salt, black pepper, and cayenne. Transfer salad to a large platter.

Lightly coat a grill or grill pan with cooking spray and heat to medium-high. Grill pork, turning frequently, until cooked through, 10 to 12 minutes. Serve warm on top of salad, and put orange wedges on the side.

Makes 4 servings

NUTRITION AT A GLANCE
Per serving: 390 calories, 20 g fat, 5 g saturated fat, 40 g protein, 13 g carbohydrate, 5 g fiber, 240 mg sodium

Middle Eastern Steak and Chickpea Salad

PREP TIME: 15 minutes   **COOK TIME:** 10 minutes   **STAND TIME:** 10 minutes

This hearty salad makes a meal in itself. In addition to or instead of the spinach, try a combination of arugula and romaine or Boston lettuce.

- 1 pound flank steak
- 1 (15.5-ounce) can chickpeas, rinsed and drained
- 4 ounces baby spinach (4 cups)
- 1 large cucumber, finely chopped
- 2 ounces reduced-fat feta cheese, crumbled (⅓ cup)
- 4 pepperoncini (from a jar)
- ½ cup parsley leaves
- ¼ cup roughly chopped fresh mint
- 1 garlic clove, minced
- 1 tablespoon fresh lemon juice
- 2 teaspoons extra-virgin olive oil

Lightly coat a grill or grill pan with cooking spray and heat to medium-high. Grill steak 4 minutes per side for medium-rare. Transfer to a cutting board and let rest for 5 to 10 minutes.

While steak is resting, in a large bowl combine chickpeas, spinach, cucumber, feta, pepperoncini, parsley, mint, garlic, lemon juice, and oil.

Slice steak thinly across the grain. Add steak and its juices to chickpea salad and toss. Serve warm or at room temperature.

Makes 4 servings

NUTRITION AT A GLANCE
Per serving: 360 calories, 14 g fat, 5 g saturated fat, 33 g protein, 25 g carbohydrate, 5 g fiber, 660 mg sodium

Grilled Steak with Texas Mop Sauce

PREP TIME: 10 minutes   **COOK TIME:** 15 minutes   **STAND TIME:** 10 minutes

Coffee might be a surprising barbecue ingredient, but in Texas it often shows up in "mop sauce," which is used to baste, or mop, meat while it's cooking, resulting in a moist and tender dish. The name probably comes from the fact that pit masters in the South actually use cotton mops to baste large quantities of slow-cooking meat. You can rub the steak with a spice mixture of your choice (see page 11 for ideas) before cooking.

½ cup no-salt-added tomato sauce

¼ cup strongly brewed decaffeinated coffee

2 tablespoons Worcestershire sauce

1 tablespoon sugar-free pancake syrup

1 (1½-pound) sirloin steak, about 1½ inches thick

1 teaspoon freshly ground black pepper

In a small saucepan, combine tomato sauce, coffee, Worcestershire sauce, and syrup. Bring to a simmer and remove from the heat. Transfer ⅔ cup of the sauce to a small bowl and reserve for dipping.

Lightly coat a grill or grill pan with cooking spray and heat to medium-high. Rub steak on both sides with pepper. Grill steak, basting frequently with remaining ⅓ cup mop sauce, 5 to 7 minutes per side for medium-rare. Allow steak to rest for 5 to 10 minutes.

Cut steak into thin slices, divide evenly among 4 plates, and serve with reserved mop sauce for dipping.

Makes 4 servings

NUTRITION AT A GLANCE
Per serving: 299 calories, 14 g fat, 5 g saturated fat, 37 g protein, 5 g carbohydrate, 0 g fiber, 180 mg sodium

Feta-Stuffed Sirloin Burgers with Sun-Dried Tomato Mayonnaise

PREP TIME: 15 minutes   COOK TIME: 10 minutes

Flavored mayonnaise is a delicious alternative to sugary ketchup for all types of burgers, whether they're made with meat, chicken, or fish. Use a vegetable peeler to get nice thin strips of crisp cucumber for topping these burgers.

Mayonnaise

- ¼ cup reduced-fat sour cream
- 8 sun-dried tomatoes in oil, drained and chopped
- 2 tablespoons mayonnaise

Burgers

- 1 pound ground sirloin
- 4 ounces reduced-fat feta cheese, crumbled (⅔ cup)
- 1 teaspoon dried oregano
- ¼ teaspoon red pepper flakes
- 4 whole-wheat or whole-grain hamburger buns, lightly toasted (optional)
- 1 small cucumber, thinly sliced

For the mayonnaise: In a small bowl, combine sour cream, tomatoes, and mayonnaise.

For the burgers: In a large bowl, combine sirloin, cheese, oregano, and pepper flakes. Form mixture into 4 patties, about ½ inch thick.

Lightly coat a large nonstick skillet with cooking spray and heat over medium-high heat. Cook burgers until browned on both sides, 3 to 4 minutes per side, or until a thermometer inserted into the thickest part registers 160°F.

Serve burgers on buns, if using, and top with mayonnaise and cucumber.

Makes 4 servings

NUTRITION AT A GLANCE

Per serving with bun: 410 calories, 19 g fat, 7 g saturated fat, 35 g protein, 26 g carbohydrate, 4 g fiber, 718 mg sodium

Per serving without bun: 290 calories, 17 g fat, 7 g saturated fat, 31 g protein, 4 g carbohydrate, 0 g fiber, 510 mg sodium

Moroccan Spice-Rubbed Pork Chops

PREP TIME: 10 minutes   **COOK TIME: 20 minutes**

Cinnamon, coriander, and cumin are mainstays of Moroccan cuisine. With these spices, plus a few pantry basics, you can quickly create a fantastic pork chop rub that's also good on chicken or meaty fish like tuna, swordfish, or bass. Try Grilled Fennel with Mixed Olives (page 83) with the pork.

2	garlic cloves, minced
1	teaspoon extra-virgin olive oil
½	teaspoon ground cinnamon
½	teaspoon ground coriander
½	teaspoon ground cumin
½	teaspoon paprika
4	(6-ounce) center rib pork chops, about ½ inch thick
¼	teaspoon salt
	Freshly ground black pepper
4	lemon wedges

In a small bowl, combine garlic, oil, cinnamon, coriander, cumin, and paprika to form a rough paste. Press spice mixture onto both sides of each pork chop.

Lightly coat a grill or grill pan with cooking spray and heat to medium-high. Grill pork until there is no trace of pink near the bone, 6 to 8 minutes per side. Sprinkle with salt and season with pepper to taste. Divide among 4 plates and serve hot with lemon wedges.

Makes 4 servings

NUTRITION AT A GLANCE
Per serving: 230 calories, 10 g fat, 3 g saturated fat, 32 g protein, 1 g carbohydrate, 0 g fiber, 210 mg sodium

Grilled Pork and Plum Salad with Almond Gremolata

PREP TIME: 20 minutes   **COOK TIME:** 25 minutes   **STAND TIME:** 10 minutes

A vibrant-tasting garnish that's often served as an accompaniment to Italian osso buco, gremolata is typically made with garlic, parsley, and lemon zest. Our version includes almonds for a wonderfully nutty flavor and extra protein.

Gremolata

- ¼ cup slivered almonds
- 1 garlic clove, peeled
- ½ cup parsley leaves
- 1 teaspoon finely grated lemon zest
- 1 teaspoon extra-virgin olive oil
- ⅛ teaspoon salt

Pork

- 2 (¾-pound) pork tenderloins
- 4 firm medium plums, halved
- 1 tablespoon extra-virgin olive oil
- 2 teaspoons red wine vinegar
- 1 teaspoon finely grated lemon zest
- ⅛ teaspoon salt
- ⅛ teaspoon freshly ground black pepper
- 6 ounces baby spinach (6 cups)

For the gremolata: In a food processor, combine almonds and garlic; pulse just until blended, about 10 seconds. Add parsley, lemon zest, oil, and salt; pulse just until blended, about 15 seconds more.

For the pork: Lightly coat a grill or grill pan with cooking spray and heat to medium-high. Grill pork 8 to 10 minutes per side, or until a thermometer inserted into the thickest part reads 150°F to 155°F. During the last 5 minutes of cooking, place plums, skin side down, on grill and cook, turning once. Transfer pork and plums to a cutting board and let pork rest for 5 to 10 minutes. While pork is resting, slice plums into wedges.

In a large bowl, combine oil, vinegar, lemon zest, salt, and pepper. Add plums and spinach and toss to combine.

Cut pork into ½-inch-thick slices. Divide pork among 4 plates and top with gremolata. Serve warm with salad.

Makes 4 servings

NUTRITION AT A GLANCE
Per serving: 340 calories, 14 g fat, 3 g saturated fat, 39 g protein, 17 g carbohydrate, 4 g fiber, 290 mg sodium

Spicy Lamb Kebabs with Cucumber-Mint Yogurt

PREP TIME: 20 minutes   **MARINATING TIME:** 20 minutes   **COOK TIME:** 15 minutes

Spice is nice, but sometimes you need a little cooldown. Mint and yogurt are the perfect pair for the job, and they're a nice complement to the cumin-based marinade that bathes these cubes of lamb before they're grilled. Use leg of lamb; it's one of the leanest and tastiest cuts.

- 1 teaspoon ground cumin
- ½ teaspoon ground coriander
- ½ teaspoon freshly ground black pepper
- ¼ teaspoon cayenne
- 1½ pounds leg of lamb, cut into 24 (1½-inch) cubes
- 4 tablespoons fresh lemon juice
- 1 teaspoon extra-virgin olive oil
- 1 cup nonfat or low-fat Greek-style plain yogurt

- 1 small cucumber, peeled, seeded, and finely chopped
- 2 tablespoons finely chopped fresh mint
- 2 garlic cloves, minced
- ½ teaspoon salt
- 2 medium red onions, cut into 16 wedges

Special equipment

- 8 (12-inch) skewers

In a large bowl, combine cumin, coriander, ¼ teaspoon of the black pepper, and cayenne. Add lamb and toss to coat. Add 3 tablespoons of the lemon juice and oil; toss again. Cover the bowl with plastic wrap and marinate lamb at room temperature for 20 minutes.

While lamb is marinating, in a medium bowl combine yogurt, cucumber, mint, garlic, salt, remaining 1 tablespoon lemon juice, and remaining ¼ teaspoon black pepper.

Lightly coat a grill or grill pan with cooking spray and heat to medium-high. Thread 3 lamb cubes and 2 onion wedges onto each skewer, alternating pieces. Grill kebabs, turning frequently, 5 to 7 minutes for medium-rare. Divide among 4 plates and serve warm with cucumber–mint yogurt.

Makes 4 (2-skewer) servings

NUTRITION AT A GLANCE
Per serving: 301 calories, 11 g fat, 4 g saturated fat, 40 g protein, 10 g carbohydrate, 1 g fiber, 420 mg sodium

VEGETARIAN'S PARADISE

With produce at its peak, summertime vegetarian meals are better than ever. The recipes on the following pages combine reduced-fat cheeses, whole-wheat pastas and tortillas, beans, tempeh, and tofu with juicy tomatoes, tender eggplant and arugula, and a host of summer herbs. Eating plenty of nutrient-rich, high-fiber carbohydrates from fruits and vegetables promotes satiety—the satisfying feeling of fullness that can help you shed pounds and maintain a weight that's right for you. You'll also get plenty of vitamins and minerals from these vegetarian delights.

Try our Spicy South Beach Diet Macaroni and Cheese, or a sweet and spicy Barbecued Tofu Wrap, or a Chicago-style "chardog"—in this case, a tofu dog prepared with a classic midwestern flair. Spaghetti with Ricotta and Fresh Tomato Sauce might become your favorite weeknight fallback. And when you're in the mood for something different, Tempeh and Vegetable Fajitas and a rich Indian Vegetable Curry are just a couple of the many dishes to choose from.

◀ *Seared Tempeh and Three-Bean Salad (page 172)*

Seared Tempeh and Three-Bean Salad

PREP TIME: 15 minutes   COOK TIME: 20 minutes

Tempeh is a flavorful soybean product that provides ample protein, fiber, and vitamins. In this warm salad, it combines with a colorful variety of beans and a handful of great summer veggies. This recipe is very flexible: You can use black beans instead of kidney and add whatever fresh vegetables you have on hand. Additional fresh herbs, like basil and cilantro, also make a good match.

2 tablespoons fresh lemon juice	1 (15-ounce) can white beans, rinsed and drained
1 tablespoon extra-virgin olive oil	12 ounces green beans, trimmed and cut into 1-inch pieces
3 teaspoons low-sodium soy sauce	1 (8-ounce) package three-grain or regular tempeh, cut into ¼-inch cubes
2 teaspoons Dijon mustard	
2 garlic cloves, minced	4 scallions, thinly sliced
⅛ teaspoon freshly ground black pepper	¼ cup chopped fresh parsley
⅛ teaspoon granular sugar substitute	1 cup cherry tomatoes, halved
1 (15-ounce) can kidney beans, rinsed and drained	

In a large bowl, whisk together lemon juice, oil, 1 teaspoon of the soy sauce, mustard, garlic, pepper, and sugar substitute. Add kidney beans and white beans; stir to combine.

Bring a large saucepan of lightly salted water to a boil. Add green beans, return to a boil, and cook until crisp-tender, about 2 minutes. Drain in a colander and immediately run under very cold water to stop cooking. Drain again and pat dry. Add to the bowl with other beans and toss to combine.

Lightly coat a large nonstick skillet with cooking spray and heat over medium-high heat. Add tempeh and remaining 2 teaspoons soy sauce. Cook, turning occasionally, until tempeh is browned on all sides, 4 to 6 minutes. Transfer tempeh to the bowl with beans and add scallions and parsley; toss to combine.

Divide salad among 4 plates, top with tomatoes, and serve warm.

Makes 4 (1⅓-cup) servings

NUTRITION AT A GLANCE
Per serving: 340 calories, 6 g fat, 1.5 g saturated fat, 19 g protein, 53 g carbohydrate, 15 g fiber, 440 mg sodium

Spaghetti with Ricotta and Fresh Tomato Sauce

PREP TIME: 10 minutes   **COOK TIME:** 20 minutes

Summer-fresh tomatoes are one of the ultimate pleasures of warm-weather dining. Here they make a tasty homemade pasta sauce that's quick and easy to prepare. Ricotta cheese adds a nice creaminess.

- 8 ounces whole-wheat spaghetti
- 6 large plum tomatoes, finely chopped
- ¾ cup part-skim ricotta cheese
- ¼ cup freshly grated Parmesan cheese
- ½ cup chopped fresh basil, plus basil leaves for garnish
- 3 garlic cloves, minced
- 2 teaspoons extra-virgin olive oil
- ¼ teaspoon salt
- ⅛ teaspoon freshly ground black pepper

Bring a large pot of lightly salted water to a boil. Add spaghetti and cook according to package directions until al dente.

While pasta is cooking, in a large bowl combine tomatoes, ricotta, Parmesan, chopped basil, and garlic.

Reserving ¼ cup of the pasta cooking liquid, drain pasta. Add pasta to the bowl with tomato mixture. Add oil, salt, and pepper; toss gently. Add reserved cooking liquid and stir to make a sauce. Garnish with basil leaves and serve warm.

Makes 4 (1½-cup) servings

NUTRITION AT A GLANCE
Per serving: 310 calories, 8 g fat, 3.5 g saturated fat, 16 g protein, 49 g carbohydrate, 8 g fiber, 300 mg sodium

Grilled Tomato, Arugula, and Feta Cheese Pizzas

PREP TIME: 10 minutes   **COOK TIME:** 5 minutes

Lovers of thin-crust pizza will like this tortilla version, as well as the grilled pizzas on pages 176 and 177 (all three are shown in the photo on the opposite page). You'll love the smoky flavor that you get from using the grill rather than the oven.

4	(8-inch) whole-wheat tortillas
4	medium plum tomatoes, thinly sliced
3½	ounces reduced-fat feta cheese, crumbled (generous ⅓ cup)
1	garlic clove, minced
2	tablespoons thinly sliced fresh basil
1⅓	cups baby arugula
2	teaspoons extra-virgin olive oil
	Salt and freshly ground black pepper

Lightly coat a grill or grill pan with cooking spray and heat to medium–high.

Grill tortillas until lightly puffed and browned on the bottom, about 1 minute. Transfer to a cutting board, grilled side up, and top tortillas evenly with tomatoes, cheese, garlic, and basil.

Return tortillas to the grill, topping side up. Cover and cook until cheese is softened, about 30 seconds. Top with arugula, cover, and grill another 1 to 2 minutes, or until arugula is wilted. Transfer pizzas to 4 plates, drizzle with oil, and season with salt and pepper. Serve warm.

Makes 4 servings

NUTRITION AT A GLANCE
Per serving: 190 calories, 8 g fat, 2.5 g saturated fat, 8 g protein, 22 g carbohydrate, 4 g fiber, 590 mg sodium

Grilled Spinach, Garlic, and Goat Cheese Pizzas

PREP TIME: 10 minutes   **COOK TIME:** 5 minutes

Tangy goat cheese is the perfect partner to the garlicky spinach on these individual pizzas. Serve them with Crisp Jícama Salad with Creamy Cilantro Dressing (page 70) for a light meal.

½ teaspoon extra-virgin olive oil

6 ounces baby spinach (6 cups)

3 garlic cloves, minced

1 tablespoon water

4 (8-inch) whole-wheat tortillas

4 medium plum tomatoes, thinly sliced

4 ounces reduced-fat goat cheese, crumbled (⅔ cup)

¼ teaspoon salt

   Freshly ground black pepper

In a large nonstick skillet, heat oil over medium heat. Add spinach and garlic; cook, stirring, about 30 seconds. Add water, cover, and reduce the heat to low. Cook until spinach is wilted, 1 to 2 minutes more.

Lightly coat a grill or grill pan with cooking spray and heat to medium-high. Grill tortillas until lightly puffed and browned on the bottom, about 1 minute. Transfer to a cutting board, grilled side up, and top tortillas evenly with tomatoes, spinach, and cheese.

Return tortillas to the grill, topping side up. Cover and cook until cheese is melted, about 1 minute. Transfer pizzas to 4 plates, sprinkle with salt, and season with pepper to taste. Serve warm.

Makes 4 servings

NUTRITION AT A GLANCE
Per serving: 180 calories, 6 g fat, 2 g saturated fat, 6 g protein, 27 g carbohydrate, 6 g fiber, 580 mg sodium

Grilled Roasted Pepper, Red Onion, and Mozzarella Pizzas

PREP TIME: 10 minutes   **COOK TIME:** 5 minutes

Buying tomato sauce and roasted peppers at the supermarket makes easy work of these crispy pizzas. Make sure to slice the onion very thin, which allows it to impart its flavor without overwhelming the rest of the toppings. Add a sprinkling of any fresh herbs you have on hand just before serving, if you like, and be sure to break out the red pepper flakes for those who prefer some heat.

4 (8-inch) whole-wheat tortillas

¼ cup canned tomato sauce

4 ounces shredded part-skim mozzarella cheese (1 cup)

½ cup roasted red pepper (from a jar), cut into ¼-inch-wide strips

½ small red onion, very thinly sliced

⅛ teaspoon salt

    Freshly ground black pepper

Lightly coat a grill or grill pan with cooking spray and heat to medium–high. Grill tortillas until lightly puffed and browned on the bottom, about 1 minute. Transfer to a cutting board, grilled side up. Spread tortillas evenly with tomato sauce and top with equal portions of cheese, red pepper, and onion.

Return pizzas to the grill, topping side up. Cover and cook until cheese is melted, about 1 minute. Transfer pizzas to 4 plates, sprinkle with salt, and season with black pepper to taste. Serve hot.

Makes 4 servings

NUTRITION AT A GLANCE

Per serving: 210 calories, 8 g fat, 3.5 g saturated fat, 10 g protein, 22 g carbohydrate, 4 g fiber, 610 mg sodium

Asian Marinated Tofu and Eggplant with Rice

PREP TIME: 15 minutes   **MARINATING TIME:** 20 minutes   **COOK TIME:** 20 minutes

Japanese and baby eggplants have a sweeter, more delicate taste than the larger American, or globe, variety, but you can use whichever is available.

- 3 tablespoons rice vinegar
- 4 garlic cloves, minced
- 1 tablespoon grated fresh ginger
- 1 tablespoon low-sodium soy sauce
- 1 teaspoon toasted sesame oil
- 1 (14-ounce) package extra-firm tofu, cut into 1-inch cubes

- 1 cup quick-cooking whole-grain brown rice
- 1 tablespoon extra-virgin olive oil
- 12 ounces Japanese or baby eggplants, cut into ½-inch cubes
- ¼ teaspoon salt
- 4 ounces snow peas, trimmed
- ¼ cup water

In a 9- by 13-inch glass baking dish, stir together vinegar, 2 teaspoons of the garlic, ginger, soy sauce, and sesame oil. Lay tofu cubes between paper towels and press to remove excess moisture. Add tofu to the baking dish with marinade and turn gently to coat well. Cover the dish with plastic wrap and marinate tofu for 20 minutes at room temperature.

While tofu is marinating, cook rice according to package directions. Remove from the heat and keep warm.

While rice is cooking, in a large nonstick skillet heat oil over medium-high heat. Add remaining garlic and cook for 1 minute. Add eggplant and salt; cook, stirring, until eggplant is browned on all sides, 4 to 5 minutes. Transfer eggplant to a large bowl.

Add snow peas and water to the skillet, cover, and cook over medium-high heat until snow peas are crisp-tender, 2 to 3 minutes. Transfer snow peas to the bowl with eggplant.

Add tofu and marinade to the skillet and cook over medium-high heat, turning with a spatula occasionally, until tofu is browned and crisped on all sides, 6 to 8 minutes. Return vegetables to the skillet and cook, gently stirring to combine with tofu, just until heated through, about 1 minute.

Divide rice among 4 plates and serve with tofu and vegetables.

Makes 4 servings

NUTRITION AT A GLANCE
Per serving: 240 calories, 12 g fat, 2 g saturated fat, 14 g protein, 21 g carbohydrate, 4 g fiber, 290 mg sodium

Indian Vegetable Curry

PREP TIME: 20 minutes   **COOK TIME: 35 minutes**

This tasty Indian-style curry has a delicious tomato-and-yogurt-based sauce. Enjoy it with brown rice on Phase 2 or 3. For a variation, add chopped fresh spinach or arugula during the last 5 minutes of cooking.

4 garlic cloves, peeled	¼ teaspoon salt
1 (2-inch) piece fresh ginger	1½ cups small cauliflower florets
1 tablespoon extra-virgin olive oil	4 ounces green beans, trimmed and cut into 1-inch pieces
1 small red onion, finely chopped	1 cup canned chickpeas, rinsed and drained
1½ teaspoons curry powder	
¾ teaspoon cumin seeds	⅓ cup water
⅛ teaspoon cayenne	1 medium zucchini, cut into ¼-inch cubes
1¼ cups canned diced tomatoes	
1 cup low-fat or nonfat plain yogurt	¼ cup finely chopped fresh cilantro

In a food processor, combine garlic and ginger; pulse until finely chopped.

In a medium saucepan, heat oil over medium-high heat. Add garlic mixture, onion, curry powder, cumin seeds, and cayenne; stir well. Reduce the heat to medium-low and cook, stirring frequently, until onion is softened, about 5 minutes.

Add tomatoes, ¾ cup of the yogurt, and salt; stir to combine. Add cauliflower, bring to a gentle simmer, and cook for 10 minutes. Add green beans, chickpeas, and water; cover and simmer for 10 minutes more. Add zucchini and continue to cook, covered, until vegetables are tender, about 8 minutes more.

Spoon curry into 4 bowls and season lightly with additional salt, if desired. Top with remaining yogurt and sprinkle with cilantro. Serve warm.

Makes 4 (1-cup) servings

NUTRITION AT A GLANCE
Per serving: 200 calories, 5 g fat, 1 g saturated fat, 9 g protein, 32 g carbohydrate, 7 g fiber, 490 mg sodium

Chicago-Style Grilled Tofu Dogs

PREP TIME: 10 minutes   **COOK TIME:** 7 minutes

The Windy City boasts its very own hot dog style that Chicagoans swear by. Essential toppings include mustard, onion, pickle relish, sliced tomatoes, jarred peppers (pepperoncini), and celery salt (which can be omitted if sodium is of concern). There's not a lick of ketchup in sight! In Chicago, hot dogs are called "chardogs" when cooked on the grill.

4   low-fat tofu hot dogs

4   whole-wheat or whole-grain hot dog buns, lightly toasted (optional)

4   teaspoons yellow mustard

1   large plum tomato, halved and thinly sliced

¼   cup no-sugar-added pickle relish

4   pepperoncini (from a jar), thinly sliced

2   tablespoons minced white onion

¼   teaspoon celery salt (optional)

Lightly coat a grill or grill pan with cooking spray and heat to medium-high. Grill hot dogs, turning frequently, until well browned on all sides, 3 to 5 minutes. Transfer hot dogs to buns, if using.

Top each hot dog with equal portions of mustard, tomato, relish, pepperoncini, and onion. Season with celery salt, if using. Serve warm.

Makes 4 servings

NUTRITION AT A GLANCE

Per serving with bun: 200 calories, 5 g fat, 1.5 g saturated fat, 12 g protein, 57 g carbohydrate, 4 g fiber, 680 mg sodium

Per serving without bun: 90 calories, 3 g fat, 1 g saturated fat, 9 g protein, 35 g carbohydrate, 0 g fiber, 570 mg sodium

Spicy South Beach Diet Macaroni and Cheese

PREP TIME: 10 minutes   **COOK TIME:** 35 minutes

Hot and bubbling from the oven, this summery version of our popular mac and cheese recipe adds fresh chopped tomatoes and basil. And a hit of cayenne turns up the volume. Look for spelt and whole-wheat pastas in health-food stores or in the pasta section of larger supermarkets.

8 ounces whole-wheat or spelt elbow pasta

1 tablespoon trans-fat-free margarine

1 tablespoon whole-wheat flour

¼ teaspoon cayenne

1¼ cups fat-free half-and-half

1 cup shredded reduced-fat sharp cheddar cheese

¼ cup chopped fresh basil

¼ teaspoon salt

2 large plum tomatoes, chopped

Freshly ground black pepper

Heat the oven to 400°F.

Bring a large saucepan of lightly salted water to a boil. Cook pasta according to package directions until al dente. Drain and rinse under cold water for 30 seconds.

While pasta is cooking, in a large nonstick skillet melt margarine over medium heat. Add flour and cayenne, reduce the heat to low, and whisk constantly until flour is incorporated, about 2 minutes.

Add half-and-half to the skillet, bring to a simmer over low heat, and cook, whisking frequently, until blended and thickened, 3 to 5 minutes. Add cheese, basil, and salt; stir until blended. Add pasta and stir until coated and warmed, about 1 minute; remove from the heat.

Lightly coat an 8- by 8-inch baking dish with cooking spray. Transfer macaroni and cheese to the baking dish. Sprinkle tomatoes on top and season with pepper. Bake until hot and bubbly, about 10 minutes. Place under the broiler and broil until the top is lightly browned, 3 to 4 minutes. Serve hot.

Makes 4 (1¼-cup) servings

NUTRITION AT A GLANCE
Per serving: 360 calories, 12 g fat, 6 g saturated fat, 18 g protein, 51 g carbohydrate, 6 g fiber, 280 mg sodium

Tofu Salad Sandwiches with Tapenade

PREP TIME: 15 minutes   MARINATING TIME: 15 minutes   COOK TIME: 10 minutes

Similar to egg salad (without the eggs!), this creamy sandwich gets extra flavor from tapenade, a puréed olive paste widely available in jars (choose sugar-free variety). If you are on Phase 1, skip the bread and enjoy the tofu salad with the roasted peppers and tapenade alongside.

  1 teaspoon dried oregano

  1 teaspoon garlic powder

  ¼ teaspoon red pepper flakes

  1 (14-ounce) package extra-firm tofu, cut into 1-inch cubes

  2 large roasted red peppers (from a jar), drained, rinsed, and roughly chopped

  12 basil leaves, roughly chopped

  2 tablespoons olive tapenade (from a jar)

  1 tablespoon mayonnaise

  8 slices thin-sliced whole-grain bread, lightly toasted (optional)

  2 cups baby arugula

In a medium bowl, combine oregano, garlic powder, and pepper flakes. Place tofu cubes between paper towels and press to remove excess moisture. Transfer tofu to the bowl with oregano mixture and stir gently to coat well. Cover the bowl with plastic wrap and marinate tofu for 15 minutes at room temperature.

Lightly coat a large nonstick skillet with cooking spray and heat over medium-high heat. Add tofu, reduce the heat to medium, and cook, gently stirring, until tofu is golden brown on all sides, about 8 minutes. Remove from the heat and transfer tofu to the original medium bowl. Add peppers and basil; stir gently with a fork to break up tofu and combine.

In a small bowl, stir together tapenade and mayonnaise. Spread tapenade mixture on 4 bread slices, if using, and top with tofu mixture, arugula, and remaining bread slices to form 4 sandwiches. Cut sandwiches in half and serve.

Makes 4 servings

NUTRITION AT A GLANCE
Per serving with bread: 239 calories, 10 g fat, 1.5 g saturated fat, 15 g protein, 22 g carbohydrate, 4 g fiber, 445 mg sodium

Per serving without bread: 170 calories, 11 g fat, 2 g saturated fat, 12 g protein, 6 g carbohydrate, 2 g fiber, 300 mg sodium

Vietnamese-Style Vegetables with Rice Noodles

PREP TIME: 20 minutes   **SOAKING TIME:** 15 minutes   **COOK TIME:** 15 minutes

This tangy and spicy dish gets its exciting flavors from chili paste, Asian fish sauce, and rice vinegar, three ingredients often used in Vietnamese cooking. For more on these ingredients, see the glossary (page 250). You can substitute 1 teaspoon low-sodium soy sauce for fish sauce, if preferred.

- 2 ounces rice noodles
- 1 tablespoon chili paste (from a jar)
- 1 tablespoon Asian fish sauce
- 1 tablespoon fresh lime juice
- 1 tablespoon rice vinegar
- 2 tablespoons extra-virgin olive oil
- 1 large head broccoli, cut into small florets (4 cups)
- 1 medium red bell pepper, thinly sliced
- 1 medium red onion, thinly sliced
- 1 medium zucchini, halved lengthwise and thinly sliced into half-moons
- ¼ cup finely chopped fresh cilantro
- 4 lime wedges

Place noodles in a medium bowl, cover with very warm tap water, and soak until softened, about 15 minutes. Drain and set aside.

While noodles are soaking, in a small bowl whisk together chili paste, fish sauce, lime juice, and vinegar.

In a large nonstick skillet, heat 1 tablespoon of the oil over medium–high heat. Add broccoli and toss to coat; cook, tossing gently, until tender, about 4 minutes. Transfer broccoli to a plate.

Add remaining 1 tablespoon oil to the skillet and heat over medium–high heat. Add pepper, onion, and zucchini; cook, stirring frequently, until vegetables are just beginning to soften, about 4 minutes. Return broccoli to the skillet and cook, stirring occasionally, for 3 minutes more. Stir in chili paste mixture, cover, and cook 1 minute more.

Add noodles to the skillet and toss well. Add cilantro and toss again. Divide among 4 plates and serve warm with lime wedges.

Makes 4 servings

NUTRITION AT A GLANCE
Per serving: 160 calories, 7 g fat, 1 g saturated fat, 4 g protein, 23 g carbohydrate, 4 g fiber, 480 mg sodium

Grilled Tempeh Burgers with Horseradish Aioli

PREP TIME: 25 minutes   **COOK TIME:** 10 minutes

Spicy horseradish aioli is the perfect topping for these moist burgers (make it in larger amounts to enjoy as a dip for crudités). Tempeh is available in all sorts of flavors, including smoked, sesame, and sea or garden vegetable. Try them all and see which you like best.

Aioli

- 2 tablespoons mayonnaise
- 1½ tablespoons prepared horseradish, drained well
- ½ teaspoon grated lemon zest
- 1 teaspoon fresh lemon juice
- 2 garlic cloves, minced

Burgers

- 4 scallions, roughly chopped
- ¼ cup roughly chopped fresh parsley
- 1 garlic clove

- 1 (8-ounce) package tempeh, crumbled
- 2 teaspoons Dijon mustard
- 1 large egg
- ¼ teaspoon salt
- ¼ teaspoon freshly ground black pepper
- 4 whole-grain hamburger buns, lightly toasted (optional)
- 4 large Boston or red leaf lettuce leaves
- 1 large plum tomato, thinly sliced

For the aioli: In a small bowl, stir together mayonnaise, horseradish, lemon zest, lemon juice, and garlic.

For the burgers: In a food processor, combine scallions, parsley, and garlic; process until finely chopped. Add tempeh, mustard, egg, salt, and pepper; pulse until mixture comes together. Form mixture into 4 patties, 1 inch thick.

Lightly coat a grill or grill pan with cooking spray and heat to medium. Grill burgers until browned and heated through, about 4 minutes per side. Place burgers on buns, if using, and top with aioli, lettuce, and tomato. Serve warm.

Makes 4 servings

NUTRITION AT A GLANCE

Per serving with bun: 330 calories, 13 g fat, 2.5 g saturated fat, 20 g protein, 32 g carbohydrate, 8 g fiber, 500 mg sodium

Per serving without bun: 180 calories, 10 g fat, 2 g saturated fat, 14 g protein, 8 g carbohydrate, 5 g fiber, 270 mg sodium

Farmers' Market Pasta Salad

PREP TIME: 15 minutes   **COOK TIME:** 25 minutes

Boasting a variety of summer vegetables, including fresh peas and corn, this flavorful pasta salad is a height-of-summer Phase 3 dish. To cut the kernels off a husked uncooked corn cob, use a sharp knife to cut the cob in half crosswise. Then stand the corn up, flat end down, and cut the kernels from the top of the cob down.

8 ounces whole-wheat fusilli	1½ cups grape tomatoes, halved
1 tablespoon extra-virgin olive oil	½ cup fresh or frozen corn kernels
1 medium red onion, finely chopped	½ cup fresh or frozen baby peas
1 large eggplant, cut into ¾-inch cubes	½ cup chopped fresh basil
½ cup water	3 tablespoons red wine vinegar
3 garlic cloves, minced	¼ teaspoon salt
1 teaspoon dried thyme	Freshly ground black pepper

Bring a large saucepan of lightly salted water to a boil. Add pasta and cook according to package directions until al dente. Drain pasta and transfer to a large bowl.

While pasta is cooking, in a large nonstick skillet heat oil over medium-high heat. Add onion, reduce the heat to medium, and cook just until softened, about 5 minutes. Add eggplant, cover, and cook, stirring occasionally, until eggplant is softened, about 8 minutes. Add water, garlic, and thyme; stir to combine. Cook, uncovered, until the pan is almost dry, about 4 minutes. Add tomatoes, corn, and peas; cook until tomatoes begin to burst, about 5 minutes. Remove from the heat and stir in basil, vinegar, and salt; season to taste with pepper.

Add vegetables to pasta and toss well. Serve warm or at room temperature.

Makes 4 (2-cup) servings

NUTRITION AT A GLANCE
Per serving: 340 calories, 6 g fat, 0.5 g saturated fat, 11 g protein, 65 g carbohydrate, 13 g fiber, 210 mg sodium

Peppery Zucchini Pasta

PREP TIME: 10 minutes **COOK TIME:** 20 minutes

When zucchini and summer squash fill the garden, we turn to this flavorful pasta dish, which can easily be doubled or tripled for a big outdoor gathering. In place of basil, try fresh cilantro, mint, regular chives, or garlic chives.

- 2 teaspoons extra-virgin olive oil
- 1 small onion, finely chopped
- 3 garlic cloves, minced
- 3 pepperoncini (from a jar), minced
- ¼ teaspoon salt
- ⅛ teaspoon freshly ground black pepper
- 8 ounces whole-wheat penne pasta
- 1 large zucchini, shredded
- 2 ounces reduced-fat goat cheese, crumbled (⅓ cup)
- 1 cup cherry or grape tomatoes, halved
- ¼ cup chopped fresh basil

In a large nonstick skillet, heat 1 teaspoon of the oil over medium–high heat. Add onion and garlic, reduce the heat to medium, and cook, stirring frequently, until onion is softened, 3 to 4 minutes. Add remaining 1 teaspoon oil, pepperoncini, salt, and pepper. Reduce the heat to low and continue cooking, stirring occasionally, for 2 to 3 minutes to flavor the oil. Remove from the heat and keep warm.

Bring a large pot of lightly salted water to a boil. Cook pasta according to package directions until al dente. Reserving 2 tablespoons of pasta cooking liquid, drain pasta.

Add pasta, reserved pasta cooking liquid, zucchini, cheese, tomatoes, and basil to skillet; toss to combine. Cook over medium heat until pasta is just heated through and cheese is melted, 1 to 2 minutes. Season with additional pepper to taste and serve warm.

Makes 4 (1½-cup) servings

NUTRITION AT A GLANCE
Per serving: 280 calories, 5 g fat, 1.5 g saturated fat, 13 g protein, 46 g carbohydrate, 6 g fiber, 400 mg sodium

Barbecued Tofu Wraps

PREP TIME: 15 minutes   **COOK TIME:** 15 minutes

Open the pantry and pull out those spices for this vegetarian barbecue dish. Shredded romaine and creamy avocado add just the right cooling touch; you can also use Savoy cabbage, if you like.

- 1 tablespoon extra-virgin olive oil
- 1 small onion, finely chopped
- 2 teaspoons garlic powder
- 2 teaspoons paprika
- 1 teaspoon mustard powder
- ½ teaspoon cayenne
- 2 tablespoons tomato paste
- 2 tablespoons Worcestershire sauce

- 1 tablespoon granular sugar substitute
- ½ cup water
- 1 (14-ounce) package extra-firm tofu, cut into cubes
- 2 teaspoons fresh lime juice
- 4 (8-inch) whole-wheat tortillas
- 3 cups shredded romaine lettuce
- 1 small avocado, sliced

In a medium skillet, heat oil over medium heat. Add onion, garlic powder, paprika, mustard, and cayenne; stir to combine. Cover and cook until onion is softened, about 5 minutes. Stir in tomato paste, Worcestershire sauce, and sugar substitute; cook, stirring, for 1 minute. Stir in water and cook 1 minute more. Add tofu, stir gently to coat with sauce, and cook until heated through, about 2 minutes. Remove from the heat, add lime juice, and stir to combine.

Warm tortillas according to package directions. Place tortillas on a cutting board. Divide lettuce, avocado, and tofu among tortillas. Fold one side of each tortilla in and roll up tortillas to form wraps. Serve warm.

Makes 4 servings

NUTRITION AT A GLANCE
Per serving: 350 calories, 19 g fat, 2.5 g saturated fat, 16 g protein, 32 g carbohydrate, 9 g fiber, 390 mg sodium

Tempeh and Vegetable Fajitas

PREP TIME: 15 minutes   **MARINATING TIME:** 30 minutes   **COOK TIME:** 20 minutes

Lime juice, garlic, and serrano pepper flavor the tasty marinade for this Tex-Mex tempeh dish. If you're a fan of fresh cilantro, chop some up to sprinkle on top just before serving. An extra squeeze of lime is also nice. Use a grill topper to keep tempeh and vegetables from falling through the grate.

¼ cup fresh lime juice

3 garlic cloves, minced

1 small serrano or jalapeño pepper, seeded and minced

3 teaspoons extra-virgin olive oil

2 teaspoons sugar-free pancake syrup

1 (8-ounce) package tempeh, cut crosswise into ¾-inch strips

2 large bell peppers, any color, cut into wide strips

1 large red onion, cut into ¼-inch-thick slices

¼ teaspoon salt

Freshly ground black pepper

4 (8-inch) whole-wheat tortillas

1 cup fresh salsa

¼ cup reduced-fat sour cream

In a 9- by 13-inch glass baking dish, whisk together lime juice, garlic, serrano pepper, 2 teaspoons of the oil, and syrup. Add tempeh, turn to coat, and arrange in a single layer. Cover the dish with plastic wrap and marinate the tempeh at room temperature for 30 minutes.

While tempeh is marinating, lightly coat a grill or grill pan with cooking spray and heat to medium-high. In a large bowl, toss bell peppers and onion with remaining 1 teaspoon oil, ⅛ teaspoon of the salt, and black pepper to taste. Grill vegetables until softened and browned, 8 to 10 minutes, turning halfway through. Transfer to a large platter.

Season tempeh with remaining ⅛ teaspoon salt and grill until lightly browned, 2 to 3 minutes per side. Transfer to the platter with the vegetables. Grill tortillas until lightly browned, about 1 minute per side.

Place 1 tortilla on each of 4 plates. Top with tempeh and grilled vegetables. Serve warm, topped with salsa and sour cream.

Makes 4 servings

NUTRITION AT A GLANCE
Per serving: 310 calories, 11 g fat, 2.5 g saturated fat, 16 g protein, 39 g carbohydrate, 9 g fiber, 740 mg sodium

SUMMERTIME SWEETS

On the South Beach Diet, desserts are not off-limits. In fact, they can be enjoyed in moderation on all phases. The sweets in this chapter are sure to satisfy. On Phase 1, the rich-tasting Iced Vanilla Coffee Milk will help you cool down on a hot day. And Creamy Lemon-Vanilla Ricotta Soufflés make an elegant choice for guests, yet they are easy enough for a more casual meal.

With fruit aplenty in the summer months, you'll find that a healthy dessert can actually help you meet your daily nutritional goals. Fruit is an excellent source of fiber, vitamins, and minerals—especially in its whole form. And when fruit is picked at the height of the season, its natural sugars allow you to use less sweetener than you would in many other desserts, and often none at all.

The treats described in the pages ahead include cherries coated with dark chocolate and rolled into decadent truffles, berries baked with a crisp topping, a velvety tiramisu, and much, much more.

◀ *South Beach Diet Tiramisu (page 196)*

South Beach Diet Tiramisu

PREP TIME: 20 minutes   COOK TIME: 20 minutes   COOL TIME: 30 minutes

A favorite Italian dessert, tiramisu (meaning "pick-me-up," in reference to the espresso and cocoa it includes) makes a light yet rich finish for summer supper.

6 large egg whites	½ cup part-skim ricotta cheese
½ teaspoon cream of tartar	½ cup fat-free or light whipped topping
⅛ teaspoon salt	
¾ teaspoon vanilla extract	¼ cup strongly brewed decaffeinated espresso
⅓ cup plus 2 teaspoons granular sugar substitute	½ teaspoon unsweetened cocoa powder
6 tablespoons whole-grain pastry flour	Mint sprigs for garnish (optional)

Heat the oven to 350°F. Lightly coat an 8- by 8-inch baking pan with cooking spray.

In a large bowl, with an electric mixer at high speed, beat egg whites, cream of tartar, and salt until soft peaks form, about 5 minutes. Add ½ teaspoon of the vanilla and beat to combine. Add ⅓ cup of the sugar substitute and beat until stiff peaks form. Sift 2 tablespoons of the flour over beaten egg whites and gently fold to incorporate. Repeat twice with remaining flour until all of the flour is incorporated.

Pour batter into the pan and gently smooth the top. Bake, turning once halfway through, until cake is golden and a tester inserted into the center comes out clean, about 20 minutes. Cool completely.

In a small bowl, combine ricotta, whipped topping, remaining 2 teaspoons sugar substitute, and remaining ¼ teaspoon vanilla. Cut cake in half vertically down the middle to make two 4- by 8-inch pieces. Place the halves on a flat work surface. Drizzle 2 tablespoons of espresso onto each half. Spread half of the ricotta mixture onto one of the halves and dust with half of the cocoa powder. Top with remaining cake half; spread the top with remaining ricotta mixture and dust with remaining cocoa powder. Using a serrated knife, gently cut cake crosswise into 4 slices and serve with mint leaves for garnish, if using.

Makes 4 servings

NUTRITION AT A GLANCE
Per serving: 130 calories, 2.5 g fat, 1.5 g saturated fat, 10 g protein, 13 g carbohydrate, 0 g fiber, 200 mg sodium

Creamy Lemon-Vanilla Ricotta Soufflés

PREP TIME: 15 minutes   **COOK TIME:** 15 minutes

These beautifully puffed sweets are an elegant twist on our classic Phase 1 ricotta crème and are just as easy to make. Measure out the ingredients ahead of time, then prepare and bake the soufflés right before serving.

1   cup part-skim ricotta cheese

2   large eggs, separated

3   tablespoons granular sugar substitute

2   teaspoons grated lemon zest

½   teaspoon lemon extract

½   teaspoon vanilla extract

    Pinch salt

Preheat the oven to 375°F. Lightly coat 4 (4-ounce) ramekins with cooking spray.

In a large bowl, whisk ricotta, egg yolks, 1 tablespoon of the sugar substitute, lemon zest, lemon extract, and vanilla until combined.

In another large bowl, with an electric mixer at high speed, beat egg whites and salt until soft peaks form, 2 to 3 minutes. Add remaining 2 tablespoons sugar substitute and continue beating until stiff peaks form. Gently fold a third of the egg whites into ricotta mixture until combined. Repeat with remaining egg whites.

Spoon ricotta mixture into prepared ramekins and bake until soufflés have risen and are set and lightly browned, about 15 minutes. Serve immediately.

Makes 4 (½-cup) servings

NUTRITION AT A GLANCE
Per serving: 130 calories, 7 g fat, 4 g saturated fat, 10 g protein, 5 g carbohydrate, 0 g fiber, 180 mg sodium

Nectarine and Plum Fans with Blue Cheese and Toasted Hazelnuts

PREP TIME: 10 minutes   **COOK TIME:** 10 minutes

This elegant yet undeniably simple dessert pairs sweet, juicy nectarines and plums with slightly salty, sharp blue cheese. The toasted hazelnuts add a pleasant crunch.

¼ cup chopped hazelnuts

2 medium nectarines, thinly sliced

2 medium plums, thinly sliced

2 ounces blue cheese, crumbled (¼ cup)

Heat the oven to 275°F. Spread hazelnuts on a baking sheet and toast, stirring once, until fragrant and golden, about 10 minutes. Transfer to a plate to cool.

Divide the nectarine and plum slices among 4 dessert plates, alternating slices in a fan shape. Sprinkle fruit evenly with blue cheese and hazelnuts. Serve at room temperature.

Makes 4 servings

NUTRITION AT A GLANCE
Per serving: 150 calories, 9 g fat, 3 g saturated fat, 5 g protein, 14 g carbohydrate, 2 g fiber, 200 mg sodium

Chocolate-Cherry Truffles

PREP TIME: 40 minutes   **COOK TIME:** 5 minutes   **CHILL TIME:** 10 minutes

These decadent confections can be made with unsweetened frozen cherries in place of fresh when cherry season starts to wane. Just defrost, drain, and gently blot them dry before using. If you're making the truffles ahead of time, lightly re-dust them with cocoa powder just before serving.

8	ounces bittersweet chocolate (preferably 70 percent or higher cocoa), finely chopped
⅓	cup fat-free half-and-half
4	ounces cherries, pitted and finely chopped (about 1 cup)
	Pinch salt
2	tablespoons unsweetened cocoa powder

Place chocolate in a heatproof medium bowl. In a small saucepan, heat half-and-half over medium heat. When it comes to a simmer, add cherries and return to a simmer. Remove from the heat and pour mixture over chocolate. Add salt and stir until chocolate is melted.

Place the bowl in the freezer until chocolate is set, about 10 minutes, removing the bowl and stirring every 2 minutes. Chocolate is ready to roll into truffles when it no longer has a pudding-like consistency and starts to harden.

Scoop out 2 teaspoons of the chocolate mixture and roll with moistened palms to form a small ball. Repeat with remaining chocolate to make 32 balls (you will need to moisten your hands more than once). If chocolate is soft, place balls in the refrigerator for 10 minutes to firm.

Place cocoa powder in a shallow dish. Roll balls in cocoa powder to coat, then roll between dry palms so that cocoa powder adheres to truffles. Serve immediately or refrigerate in an airtight container for up to 1 week.

Makes 16 (2-piece) servings

NUTRITION AT A GLANCE
Per serving: 80 calories, 6 g fat, 3 g saturated fat, 1 g protein, 9 g carbohydrate, 1 g fiber, 25 mg sodium

Star Anise-Spiced Fruit Skewers

PREP TIME: 15 minutes   **COOK TIME:** 15 minutes

Aptly named, star anise is a star-shaped spice with a light anise flavor; it is commonly used in Chinese cuisine. The whole spice can be ground using a spice grinder or coffee mill; if you use a coffee mill, simply clean it by grinding a few cubes of bread before and after grinding the anise. You can also purchase preground star anise.

16	medium strawberries
½	medium mango, peeled and cut into 8 cubes
½	cup water
¼	cup granular sugar substitute
2	star anise, ground (½ teaspoon)

Special equipment

8 (6-inch) skewers

Thread 2 strawberries and 1 mango cube onto each skewer. Lightly coat a grill or grill pan with cooking spray and heat to medium.

In a small saucepan, combine water, sugar substitute, and star anise; bring to a simmer and cook until thickened to a syrupy consistency, 5 to 7 minutes.

Brush fruit with syrup and grill, turning occasionally, until fruit is lightly browned and starting to soften, about 5 minutes. Serve warm.

Makes 4 (2-skewer) servings

NUTRITION AT A GLANCE
Per serving: 50 calories, 0 g fat, 0 g saturated fat, 1 g protein, 13 g carbohydrate, 2 g fiber, 0 mg sodium

Iced Vanilla Coffee Milk

PREP TIME: 15 minutes

Whipped topping turns this Phase 1 coffee milk into a satisfying, rich-tasting dessert. The cinnamon stick stirrer adds a light spiced flavor. You can also sprinkle some ground cinnamon on top, if you like.

3	cups strongly brewed decaffeinated coffee, chilled
1	cup fat-free or 1% milk
2	teaspoons vanilla extract
2	teaspoons granular sugar substitute
	Ice cubes
½	cup fat-free or light whipped topping
	Pinch ground cinnamon for garnish (optional)
4	cinnamon sticks for garnish (optional)

In a pitcher, combine coffee, milk, vanilla, and sugar substitute; stir well. Fill 4 (10-ounce) glasses with ice. Pour coffee mixture over ice. Spoon 2 tablespoons of the whipped topping into each glass. Stir gently so that some topping mixes with coffee and some remains at the top of the glass. Garnish each with a pinch of ground cinnamon and a cinnamon stick, if using.

Makes 4 (1-cup) servings

NUTRITION AT A GLANCE
Per serving: 50 calories, 0 g fat, 0 g saturated fat, 2 g protein, 6 g carbohydrate, 0 g fiber, 45 mg sodium

Raspberry Ices

PREP TIME: 10 minutes   COOK TIME: 5 minutes   CHILL TIME: 2 hours

Vibrant in color and packed with fiber and antioxidants, raspberries are delicious in these refreshing, fruity ices. Use less sugar substitute if you like a more tart dessert.

1½ cups water

½ cup granular sugar substitute

2 pints raspberries

2 teaspoons grated lemon zest

Pinch salt

Mint sprigs for garnish (optional)

Special equipment

2 standard ice cube trays

In a small saucepan, bring water and sugar substitute to a boil; turn off the heat. Add raspberries and mash with a fork, leaving small chunks of fruit. Stir in lemon zest and salt. Pour mixture into ice cube trays and freeze until nearly frozen, about 2 hours.

Transfer raspberry cubes to a blender or food processor and pulse briefly (do not overmix or you will have a liquid drink). If the mixture starts to melt before serving, place in a bowl in the freezer and stir frequently until it reaches the desired consistency. Serve immediately, garnished with mint sprigs if desired.

Makes 4 (½-cup) servings

NUTRITION AT A GLANCE

Per serving: 80 calories, 1 g fat, 0 g saturated fat, 1 g protein, 18 g carbohydrate, 8 g fiber, 75 mg sodium

Cool-Down-Quick Peach Pops

PREP TIME: 10 minutes   **CHILL TIME: 4 hours**

Pairing fresh basil with fruit makes a delicious and sophisticated hot-weather dessert. The herb is optional—kids will probably prefer their pops without. This recipe doubles easily, so you can have plenty on hand for those sweltering days.

4 medium peaches, peeled and cubed

½ cup water

2 tablespoons granular sugar substitute

1 cup nonfat or low-fat plain yogurt

2 tablespoons chopped fresh basil (optional)

Special equipment

12 (3-ounce) paper cups

12 wooden sticks for pops

In a blender, purée peaches and water until smooth. Add sugar substitute, yogurt, and basil, if using, and blend until combined.

Divide mixture evenly among the paper cups and insert a wooden stick into the center of each. Place pops in the freezer for 4 hours or overnight. When ready to serve, peel off paper cups.

Makes 12 servings

NUTRITION AT A GLANCE
Per serving: 20 calories, 0 g fat, 0 g saturated fat, 1 g protein, 5 g carbohydrate, 0 g fiber, 10 mg sodium

Fresh Blackberry Tartlets

PREP TIME: 10 minutes   **COOK TIME:** 5 minutes   **COOL TIME:** 5 minutes

These pretty summer tartlets can easily be prepared ahead. The filling can be made up to 12 hours in advance and kept covered in the refrigerator, and the tarts can be filled up to 1 hour before serving. Look for mini phyllo tart shells in your supermarket's freezer section; they defrost in just 10 minutes. For easier cleanup, line the baking sheet with parchment.

12	frozen mini phyllo tart shells, defrosted
15	blackberries
¾	cup fat-free or light whipped topping
1	teaspoon fresh lemon juice
¼	teaspoon vanilla extract

Heat the oven to 350°F. Arrange tart shells on a baking sheet and bake until crisp, 3 to 5 minutes. Allow to cool before filling, about 5 minutes.

Set aside 12 blackberries for topping the tarts. Place remaining blackberries in a small bowl and mash with a fork. Add whipped topping and stir to combine. Stir in lemon juice and vanilla.

Spoon 1 tablespoon of the whipped topping mixture into each tart shell. Top each tart with a blackberry and serve.

Makes 4 (3-piece) servings

NUTRITION AT A GLANCE
Per serving: 100 calories, 3 g fat, 0 g saturated fat, 2 g protein, 13 g carbohydrate, 2 g fiber, 30 mg sodium

Floating Caribbean Islands

PREP TIME: 20 minutes   **COOK TIME:** 10 minutes

Floating island (or île flottante*) is a French dessert made up of a light meringue "island" floating on a sea of sweet sauce. Red and golden raspberries and tiny cantaloupe balls make a dramatic visual presentation (use just red berries if you can't find golden). When baking the meringues, be sure to use nonstick foil or parchment— or lightly coat regular foil with nonstick spray—to ensure that the meringues will not stick.*

½ cup unsweetened shredded coconut

2 cups cantaloupe cubes plus ½ cup tiny cantaloupe balls (about 2½-pound melon)

2 small bananas, sliced

1 cup nonfat or low-fat plain yogurt

3 large egg whites

Pinch salt

½ cup granular sugar substitute

½ cup red raspberries

½ cup golden raspberries

Heat the oven to 275°F. Spread coconut on a baking sheet and toast until golden, 4 to 5 minutes. Transfer to a plate to cool.

Line another baking sheet with parchment paper or nonstick foil and increase the oven temperature to 450°F.

In a blender, purée cubed cantaloupe, bananas, and yogurt until smooth; set aside.

In a large bowl, with an electric mixer at high speed, beat egg whites and salt until soft peaks form, 2 to 3 minutes. Add sugar substitute and continue beating until stiff peaks form; fold in coconut. Spoon egg white mixture into 4 mounds on baking sheet. Bake until lightly golden, about 5 minutes. Meringues should be slightly crisp and very lightly browned on the outside.

Divide reserved fruit purée among 4 shallow bowls. Using a spatula, transfer a meringue to the center of each bowl. Arrange a few cantaloupe balls and some raspberries decoratively around each meringue and serve.

Makes 4 servings

NUTRITION AT A GLANCE
Per serving: 200 calories, 7 g fat, 5 g saturated fat, 8 g protein, 33 g carbohydrate, 6 g fiber, 170 mg sodium

Strawberry-Blueberry Crunch

PREP TIME: 10 minutes   **COOK TIME:** 35 minutes

This warm baked fruit dessert topped with fresh ricotta requires little effort. It's the perfect treat for the Fourth of July, with colors that aptly suit America's birthday bash theme.

- ¼ cup whole almonds plus 2 tablespoons sliced almonds
- ¼ teaspoon ground cinnamon
- ¼ teaspoon freshly ground nutmeg
- 1 tablespoon trans-fat-free margarine
- 2 cups sliced strawberries
- 1 cup blueberries
- 1 tablespoon granular sugar substitute
- 6 tablespoons part-skim ricotta cheese

Preheat the oven to 350°F.

In a blender or spice grinder, grind whole almonds until finely ground. In a small bowl, combine ground almonds, cinnamon, and nutmeg. Add margarine and stir to combine.

Lightly coat an 8- by 8-inch baking dish with cooking spray. Place strawberries, blueberries, and sugar substitute in the dish; toss to combine. Dot with ground nut mixture (it will not cover entire surface) and then sprinkle with sliced almonds.

Bake for 35 minutes, or until topping is golden and fruit is hot. Divide fruit among 6 dessert bowls and top each serving with 1 tablespoon of ricotta.

Makes 6 (generous ½-cup) servings

NUTRITION AT A GLANCE
Per serving: 100 calories, 6 g fat, 1.5 g saturated fat, 4 g protein, 10 g carbohydrate, 3 g fiber, 35 mg sodium

Peach-Almond Parfaits

PREP TIME: 15 minutes   **COOK TIME:** 10 minutes

Making this dessert in parfait glasses or beautiful dessert bowls adds to the fun, especially for kids, because you can see all the tasty layers you're about to enjoy.

¼	cup slivered almonds
⅔	cup part-skim ricotta cheese
⅔	cup low-fat or nonfat plain yogurt
2	tablespoons granular sugar substitute
3	medium peaches, cubed (2 cups)
	Ground cinnamon

Heat the oven to 275°F. Spread almonds on a baking sheet and toast, stirring occasionally, until fragrant and golden, about 10 minutes. Transfer to a plate to cool.

In a blender or food processor, combine ricotta, yogurt, and sugar substitute and process until smooth. Spoon ¼ cup of the peaches into each of 4 parfait glasses or dessert dishes. Spoon 2 tablespoons of the ricotta mixture over the peaches. Sprinkle with a pinch of cinnamon and ½ tablespoon of the almonds. Top evenly with remaining peaches, remaining ricotta mixture, a pinch of cinnamon, and remaining almonds.

Makes 4 (1-cup) servings

NUTRITION AT A GLANCE
Per serving: 160 calories, 8 g fat, 2.5 g saturated fat, 9 g protein, 15 g carbohydrate, 2 g fiber, 80 mg sodium

Summer Fruit Cocktail

PREP TIME: 15 minutes

There's nothing like a bowl of fresh, juicy peaches and plump berries to make summer feel like it could last forever. These seasonal fruits provide a nice dose of fiber as well as vitamin C and other antioxidants.

- 2 medium peaches, cubed
- ⅔ cup blueberries
- 5 medium strawberries, sliced
- 2 teaspoons fresh lemon juice
- 1 teaspoon granular sugar substitute
- 1 tablespoon sliced fresh mint

In a large bowl, gently combine peaches, blueberries, and strawberries. Add lemon juice and sugar substitute; toss gently. Divide fruit among 4 bowls, sprinkle with mint, and serve.

Makes 4 (¾-cup) servings

NUTRITION AT A GLANCE
Per serving: 45 calories, 0 g fat, 0 g saturated fat, 1 g protein, 11 g carbohydrate, 2 g fiber, 0 mg sodium

Plum Rice Pudding

PREP TIME: 5 minutes   **COOK TIME:** 10 minutes

Warm and creamy, this quick-cooking plum-y pudding is a great dessert for cooler summer eves. Since plums are available from May through October and come in an amazingly diverse range of types, you can enjoy this recipe several times throughout the season, with countless flavor variations. Red-skinned sweet Casselmans, tart Damsons, yellow-fleshed Greengages, and even hybrids like the pluot (plum-apricot) are just a few of the many delicious plums you may find.

> 1 tablespoon slivered almonds
>
> 2 cups cooked whole-grain brown rice
>
> 1¼ cups fat-free half-and-half
>
> 1 tablespoon plus 1 teaspoon granular sugar substitute
>
> 1 teaspoon vanilla extract
>
> 2 small plums, thinly sliced
>
> 1 teaspoon ground cinnamon

Heat the oven to 275°F. Spread almonds on a baking sheet and toast, stirring once, until fragrant and golden, about 7 minutes. Transfer to a plate to cool.

While almonds are toasting, in a medium saucepan bring rice, half-and-half, sugar substitute, and vanilla to a simmer over medium heat, stirring occasionally. Add plums and cinnamon; cook until liquid is absorbed and plums are softened, about 8 minutes. Transfer pudding to 4 dessert bowls, sprinkle evenly with almonds, and serve hot.

Makes 4 (⅔-cup) servings

NUTRITION AT A GLANCE
Per serving: 210 calories, 3 g fat, 0.5 g saturated fat, 6 g protein, 39 g carbohydrate, 3 g fiber, 115 mg sodium

REFRESHING DRINKS

With temperatures on the rise and increased time spent outdoors—whether you're biking, hiking, boating, gardening, or enjoying the beach—getting plenty of liquids is a must. The refreshing drinks in this chapter make it easy to keep your body hydrated without the empty calories you find in many store-bought soft drinks and packaged juices.

Try your hand at a natural soda, like a Raspberry-Grape Sparkler, which combines blended fresh fruits with bubbly chilled seltzer. Brew up a pitcher or two of cooling iced green or hibiscus tea to drink on the porch or take to a picnic. Or invite a few friends for "mocktails." Intensely flavored and made without alcohol, these sophisticated beverages can be sipped on their own or paired with food. Iced Pom-Mojito Spritzers, for example, are a great match for the many Latin American– and Caribbean-inspired dishes in this book. There are also drinks, like our Peach-Raspberry Shake and decadent Chilly Chocolate, that double as a satisfying snack or dessert.

◀ *Cran-gria (page 216)*

Cran-gria

PREP TIME: 15 minutes   **STEEP TIME:** 30 minutes

This delicious twist on the Spanish classic, sangria, is refreshing and fruity. Serve Cran-gria from a clear pitcher or punch bowl and use globe-shaped wineglasses to show off the fruit.

- 1¼ cups unsweetened cranberry juice
- 1 cup blueberries, roughly chopped
- 1 peach, thinly sliced
- 3 tablespoons granular sugar substitute
- 1 lime, thinly sliced
- 1½ cups chilled seltzer water
- Ice cubes

In a large pitcher, combine cranberry juice, blueberries, peach, sugar substitute, and lime; stir well to dissolve sugar substitute. Let mixture sit at room temperature until flavors blend, about 30 minutes. Add seltzer and stir to combine.

Fill 4 (10-ounce) glasses with ice cubes. Pour Cran-gria over ice, add a few pieces of fruit from the pitcher to each glass, and serve.

Makes 4 (1-cup) servings

NUTRITION AT A GLANCE
Per serving: 80 calories, 0 g fat, 0 g saturated fat, 1 g protein, 22 g carbohydrate, 2 g fiber, 0 mg sodium

Orange Gingerade

PREP TIME: 15 minutes   STEEP TIME: 10 minutes

Antioxidant-rich fresh ginger lends an invigorating, slightly peppery flavor to this tasty drink. In wintertime, when there is a wide variety of orange types available, try making this drink with Cara Cara or blood oranges; both add extra sweetness and vibrant color.

1½ cups water

4 ounces fresh ginger, peeled and roughly chopped (1 cup)

2 large seedless oranges, peeled and roughly chopped

Ice cubes

3 tablespoons granular sugar substitute

In a small saucepan, bring water to a boil and remove from the heat. Add ginger and steep for 10 minutes. While ginger is steeping, in a blender, purée oranges until smooth.

Strain steeped ginger water into a large pitcher; discard ginger. Add 1 cup ice cubes and sugar substitute to ginger water and stir until ice has melted and ginger water has cooled, about 3 minutes. Add puréed oranges and stir to combine.

Fill 4 (8-ounce) glasses with ice cubes; pour Orange Gingerade over ice and serve.

Makes 4 (¾-cup) servings

NUTRITION AT A GLANCE
Per serving: 40 calories, 0 g fat, 0 g saturated fat, 1 g protein, 10 g carbohydrate, 2 g fiber, 0 mg sodium

Mango Lassi

PREP TIME: 10 minutes

A frothy and refreshing yogurt drink, lassi hails from India, where it is often made with fruits such as mango. Try it with Indian Vegetable Curry (page 180) or as a satisfying morning or afternoon snack. A pinch of the ground spice cardamom adds a uniquely sweet and pungent flavor.

- 1 medium mango, peeled and roughly chopped
- 1½ cups low-fat or nonfat plain yogurt
- ½ cup chilled water
- 1 tablespoon granular sugar substitute

  Pinch ground cardamom (optional)

  Ice cubes

In a blender, combine mango, yogurt, water, sugar substitute, and cardamom, if using; purée until smooth. Fill 4 (8-ounce) glasses with ice cubes. Pour Mango Lassi over ice and serve.

Makes 4 (¾-cup) servings

NUTRITION AT A GLANCE
Per serving: 80 calories, 1 g fat, 0.5 g saturated fat, 4 g protein, 15 g carbohydrate, 0 g fiber, 50 mg sodium

Chilly Chocolate

PREP TIME: 5 minutes

This chocolate-lover's treat is made extra-special with a touch of vanilla extract. Tasty variations are endless. Try adding other extracts, such as peppermint, cherry, almond, coconut, raspberry, or banana.

3 tablespoons unsweetened cocoa powder

2 tablespoons granular sugar substitute

Pinch salt

3 cups cold 1% milk

½ teaspoon vanilla extract

Ice cubes

In a medium bowl, stir together cocoa powder, sugar substitute, and salt. Slowly pour in 1 cup of the milk and whisk until smooth. Whisk in remaining 2 cups milk and vanilla.

Fill 4 (8-ounce) glasses with ice. Pour Chilly Chocolate over ice and serve.

Makes 4 (¾-cup) servings

NUTRITION AT A GLANCE

Per serving: 90 calories, 2.5 g fat, 1.5 g saturated fat, 7 g protein, 12 g carbohydrate, 1 g fiber, 95 mg sodium

Ocean Breezes

PREP TIME: 10 minutes

This bubbly fruit punch makes you feel like you're on the beach, no matter where you are. Using both the flesh and the juice of fruits like grapefruit ensures that you get all of the vitamins plus the fiber.

½ large pink or red grapefruit, peeled and roughly chopped

½ cup unsweetened cranberry juice

2 tablespoons fresh lime juice

1 tablespoon granular sugar substitute

2 cups chilled sugar-free cranberry seltzer water

4 lime wedges

In a blender, combine grapefruit, cranberry juice, lime juice, and sugar substitute; purée until smooth. Slowly add seltzer and stir gently with a wooden spoon to blend. Pour Ocean Breezes into 4 large martini glasses, garnish with lime wedges, and serve.

Makes 4 (1-cup) servings

NUTRITION AT A GLANCE
Per serving: 30 calories, 0 g fat, 0 g saturated fat, 0 g protein, 8 g carbohydrate, 0 g fiber, 0 mg sodium

Mary on the Beach

PREP TIME: 10 minutes

Canned whole tomatoes add a deliciously pure and super-concentrated tomato flavor to this variation on a favorite brunch cocktail. In a rush? You can substitute 3 cups low-sodium tomato juice, if you like. Or, if you're a gardener, try making this Mary with fresh tomato juice: Use the ripest tomatoes whirled in a juicer.

1	(28-ounce) can whole peeled tomatoes, with juices
1	cup chilled water
⅓	cup fresh lemon juice
1	tablespoon Worcestershire sauce
1	teaspoon hot pepper sauce
¼	teaspoon celery seeds
¼	teaspoon freshly ground black pepper
	Ice cubes
4	celery stalks, with leaves
4	lime wedges

In a blender, purée tomatoes and their juices until smooth. Strain purée into a large pitcher, pushing liquid through the strainer with a rubber spatula; discard seeds. Add water, lemon juice, Worcestershire sauce, hot pepper sauce, celery seeds, and pepper to the pitcher; stir to combine.

Fill 4 (10-ounce) glasses with ice. Pour tomato mixture over ice, add a celery stalk and lime wedge to each glass, and serve.

Makes 4 (1-cup) servings

NUTRITION AT A GLANCE
Per serving: 45 calories, 0 g fat, 0 g saturated fat, 2 g protein, 11 g carbohydrate, 2 g fiber, 340 mg sodium

Calypso Coolers

PREP TIME: 10 minutes

Almonds add protein and extra "island" flavor to this thick, rich tropical treat. Peel and freeze several bananas ahead of time so that you can make this drink at a moment's notice. They will keep in a tightly sealed freezer bag for up to 3 months.

¼ cup sliced almonds

1 cup chilled water

1 banana, peeled and frozen

1 cup low-fat or nonfat plain yogurt

1 tablespoon fresh lime juice

1 teaspoon vanilla extract

Ice cubes

4 large strawberries for garnish (optional)

In a blender, purée almonds and water until almonds are very finely chopped. Cut banana into chunks and add to blender; purée until mixture is thick. Add yogurt, lime juice, and vanilla; purée until smooth.

Fill 4 (8-ounce) glasses with ice. Pour Calypso Coolers over ice, garnish with strawberries, if using, and serve.

Makes 4 (¾-cup) servings

NUTRITION AT A GLANCE
Per serving: 100 calories, 4 g fat, 1 g saturated fat, 5 g protein, 13 g carbohydrate, 1 g fiber, 45 mg sodium

Iced Green Sun Tea

PREP TIME: 5 minutes   **STEEP TIME:** 1 hour   **CHILL TIME:** 20 minutes

Fans of sun tea believe that steeping tea slowly in the sun makes a less bitter brew. Place the tea in the sunniest window you have or on a sunny deck or patio. Once made, it will keep in the refrigerator for several days. We've chosen antioxidant-rich green tea, but you can make sun tea with any regular or herbal tea. Try adding sprigs of an aromatic herb (see page 7), but remove them before refrigerating.

4 green tea bags

4 cups water

   Ice cubes

   Granular sugar substitute to taste (optional)

1 small lemon, sliced

4 mint sprigs for garnish (optional)

Place tea bags in a large glass jar or pitcher. Pour water over bags, cover the jar with plastic wrap, and place on a sun-filled windowsill or outside during the hottest part of the day. Steep until tea is light green and flavorful, about 1 hour.

Remove tea bags from the jar and discard. Refrigerate tea to cool, about 20 minutes. Fill 4 (10-ounce) glasses with ice. Pour tea over ice, add sugar substitute, if using, garnish with lemon slices and mint sprigs, if using, and serve.

Makes 4 (1-cup) servings

NUTRITION AT A GLANCE
Per serving: 0 calories, 0 g fat, 0 g saturated fat, 0 g protein, 0 g carbohydrate, 0 g fiber, 5 mg sodium

Raspberry-Grape Sparklers

PREP TIME: 10 minutes

When temperatures rise, reach for this refreshing, healthy pick-me-up. Its two main ingredients, red grapes and raspberries, provide a double hit of vitamin C. Try it with strawberries in place of raspberries and add fresh mint, if you like.

1 cup seedless red grapes (30 grapes)

1 cup raspberries

Ice cubes

2 cups chilled seltzer water

In a blender, combine grapes and raspberries; purée until smooth. Strain mixture into a large pitcher (you should have about 1 cup); discard seeds.

Fill 4 (8-ounce) glasses with ice. Pour ¼ cup of fruit mixture into each glass and top with seltzer. Stir gently and serve.

Makes 4 (¾-cup) servings

NUTRITION AT A GLANCE
Per serving: 50 calories, 0 g fat, 0 g saturated fat, 1 g protein, 12 g carbohydrate, 3 g fiber, 0 g sodium

Strawberry-Citrus Refreshers

PREP TIME: 15 minutes

This pretty drink looks especially nice when you use the reserved strawberries as a garnish for the glasses. Cut each berry halfway up from the tip toward the cap and then neatly fit one onto the rim of each glass. The sweetest strawberries are often the smaller, bright red ones you may find at farm stands or farmers' markets at the height of your local season.

         1 pint strawberries

         1 large seedless orange, peeled and roughly chopped

         2 tablespoons fresh lime juice

         1 tablespoon granular sugar substitute

        1½ cups chilled water

            Ice cubes

Set 4 small strawberries aside for garnish; hull the rest. In a blender, combine hulled strawberries, orange, lime juice, and sugar substitute; purée until smooth. Stir in water.

   Fill 4 (10-ounce) glasses with ice cubes. Pour Strawberry-Citrus Refreshers over ice, garnish with reserved strawberries, and serve.

Makes 4 (1-cup) servings

NUTRITION AT A GLANCE
Per serving: 45 calories, 0 g fat, 0 g saturated fat, 1 g protein, 11 g carbohydrate, 2 g fiber, 0 mg sodium

Iced Pom-Mojito Spritzers

PREP TIME: 15 minutes

Pomegranates have one of the highest antioxidant contents of all fruits and vegetables. This refreshing drink puts a healthy twist on the popular Cuban mojito cocktail. Serve it with Caribbean-style dishes, like Jerk Chicken with Cool Romaine Salad (page 144), or just enjoy it on its own.

½	cup mint leaves, plus 4 mint sprigs for garnish
1½	tablespoons granular sugar substitute
2	tablespoons fresh lime juice, plus 4 lime slices for garnish
1	cup unsweetened 100% pomegranate juice
2	cups chilled sugar-free cranberry seltzer water
	Ice cubes

In the bottom of a large pitcher, using a muddler or a large wooden spoon, mash mint leaves and sugar substitute together until mint is crushed. Add lime juice and continue to crush. Add pomegranate juice and seltzer; stir gently to combine.

Fill 4 (10-ounce) glasses with ice cubes. Pour Pom–Mojitos Spritzers over ice, adding a few mint leaves from the pitcher. Garnish with lime slices and mint sprigs and serve.

Makes 4 (1-cup) servings

NUTRITION AT A GLANCE
Per serving: 50 calories, 0 g fat, 0 g saturated fat, 1 g protein, 11 g carbohydrate, 0 g fiber, 15 mg sodium

Peach-Raspberry Shakes

PREP TIME: 10 minutes

Fruity and filling, this shake can be made with any combination of berries and peaches or with nectarines or plums instead of peaches. Have it as a snack or dessert, if you prefer.

> 3 small peaches, sliced
>
> 1 cup low-fat or nonfat plain yogurt
>
> 1 cup 1% milk
>
> 1 cup raspberries
>
> 2 ice cubes
>
> 1 teaspoon vanilla extract
>
> Granular sugar substitute to taste (optional)

In a blender, combine peaches, yogurt, milk, raspberries, ice cubes, and vanilla; purée until smooth. Add sugar substitute to taste, if using. Pour into 4 (10-ounce) glasses and serve.

Makes 4 (1-cup) servings

NUTRITION AT A GLANCE
Per serving: 110 calories, 2 g fat, 1 g saturated fat, 6 g protein, 17 g carbohydrate, 3 g fiber, 75 mg sodium

Hibiscus Tea Spritzers with Lime

PREP TIME: 5 minutes   **STEEP TIME:** 6 minutes   **CHILL TIME:** 10 minutes

Hibiscus is a tropical flower that is often used to make delicious herbal teas. Its fruity, lightly floral taste and stunning red color are reminiscent of cranberries. Rich in vitamin C and antioxidants, hibiscus has also been found to be a natural relaxant. In this recipe, you can use 100% hibiscus tea or one of the many herbal blends containing hibiscus.

2 cups water

4 hibiscus tea bags

   Ice cubes

1½ cups chilled sugar-free lime seltzer water

   Granular sugar substitute to taste (optional)

1 small lime, sliced

In a small saucepan, bring water to a boil. Remove the saucepan from the heat, add tea bags, and steep for 6 minutes. Stir in 1 cup ice cubes and refrigerate until cooled, about 10 minutes.

Fill 4 (10-ounce) glasses with ice. Pour tea over ice, top with seltzer, add sugar substitute, if using, and stir gently. Garnish with lime slices and serve.

Makes 4 (1-cup) servings

NUTRITION AT A GLANCE
Per serving: 0 calories, 0 g fat, 0 g saturated fat, 0 g protein, 0 g carbohydrate, 0 g fiber, 0 mg sodium

Melon Agua Fresca Slushes

PREP TIME: 15 minutes   **FREEZING TIME: 1 to 2 hours**

Agua fresca (Spanish for "fresh water") is a refreshing Latin American drink that combines puréed sweet fruits with other ingredients, such as citrus juice, cucumber, and tamarind. Our thick, slushy version combines juicy honeydew melon and lime and is particularly welcome on a hot summer day.

1	(5-pound) honeydew melon, peeled and roughly chopped (8 cups)
½	cup chilled water
2	tablespoons fresh lime juice
2	tablespoons granular sugar substitute
1	cup ice cubes
1	small lime, thinly sliced

Spread melon pieces on a baking sheet and freeze for 1 to 2 hours, until just barely frozen.

In a blender or food processor, combine frozen melon, water, and lime juice; blend until smooth. Add sugar substitute and ice cubes and continue to process until thick and slushy.

Divide Agua Fresca Slushes among 4 (8-ounce) glasses, garnish with lime slices, and serve.

Makes 4 (¾-cup) servings

NUTRITION AT A GLANCE
Per serving: 130 calories, 0 g fat, 0 g saturated fat, 2 g protein, 32 g carbohydrate, 3 g fiber, 60 mg sodium

HOW TO EAT ON PHASE 1

On the following pages, you will find a week of sample meal plans for Phase 1, created in part with recipes from this book. Use these meal plans as guidelines, then make up your own menus for all 14 days of Phase 1.

Keep in mind that the South Beach Diet doesn't require you to measure what you eat in ounces, calories, or anything else. Weighing, measuring, and counting are certainly not conducive to a pleasant lifestyle, and it is an approach you're unlikely to sustain. It is also unnecessary. Generally, if you are making the right food choices, portion control takes care of itself. Your meals should be of normal size—enough to satisfy your hunger. And while you should never leave a meal hungry, that doesn't mean that you must clean your plate. Try to eat slowly so that your brain has time to detect your normal rise in blood sugar. This becomes much easier once you have completed Phase 1 and cravings, especially for sweets, baked goods, and other refined starches, have largely disappeared. (See page 3 for more information.)

While we don't generally recommend weighing and measuring on the South Beach Diet, there are a couple of exceptions: We do recommend that you eat a minimum of 2 cups of vegetables with lunch and dinner so you get the maximum antioxidant and fiber benefits, and we also suggest that you get 2 cups of nonfat or low-fat dairy (including yogurt) each day. Also remember to drink water throughout the day to stay well hydrated.

DAY 1

BREAKFAST

6 ounces vegetable juice cocktail

Poached Eggs with Cherry Tomatoes and Scallions (page 28)

2 slices turkey bacon

Coffee with 1% or fat-free milk and sugar substitute

MIDMORNING SNACK

Celery stuffed with 1 wedge reduced-fat spreadable cheese

LUNCH

Curried Chicken Salad with Peanuts (page 136) on a bed of Bibb lettuce

Red, yellow, green, and orange bell pepper strips with Horseradish Aioli (page 188)

Sugar-free Popsicle

MIDAFTERNOON SNACK

Hummus with vegetable dippers

DINNER

Mixed Seafood Kebabs with Parsley-Garlic Sauce (page 109)

Savoy Slaw with Sesame Dressing (page 88)

DESSERT

Chilly Chocolate (page 220)

DAY 2

BREAKFAST

6 ounces tomato juice

Scrambled eggs with smoked salmon

Sliced tomatoes, sliced onions, and capers

Coffee or tea with 1% or fat-free milk and sugar substitute

MIDMORNING SNACK

Fat-free black bean dip with crudités

LUNCH

Grilled Southwest Steak, Radish, and Blue Cheese Salad (page 72)

Iced Green Sun Tea (page 225)

Sugar-free flavored gelatin dessert

MIDAFTERNOON SNACK

½ cup shelled edamame

DINNER

Quick Chicken Tagine (page 134)

Watercress salad with lemon vinaigrette

DESSERT

4 ounces nonfat or low-fat plain yogurt with a splash of vanilla extract and a sprinkling of sugar substitute

DAY 3

BREAKFAST

6 ounces vegetable juice cocktail

Energy shake (artificially sweetened vanilla low-fat soy milk, low-fat plain yogurt, tofu, and a few almonds)

Coffee or tea with 1% or fat-free milk and sugar substitute

MIDMORNING SNACK

5 part-skim mozzarella balls with sugar-free balsamic vinaigrette

LUNCH

Fresh Blackened Tuna with Greens (page 97)

Mary on the Beach (page 222)

Sugar-free popsicle

MIDAFTERNOON SNACK

4 ounces 1% cottage cheese with grape tomatoes

DINNER

Grilled Steak with Texas Mop Sauce (page 163)

Grilled Chipotle Onion Rings (page 84)

Crisp Jícama Salad with Creamy Cilantro Dressing (page 70)

DESSERT

Creamy Lemon-Vanilla Ricotta Soufflé (page 197)

DAY 4

BREAKFAST

6 ounces vegetable juice cocktail

Summer Squash Scramble with Fresh Tomato (page 17)

2 slices Canadian bacon

Coffee or tea with 1% or fat-free milk and sugar substitute

MIDMORNING SNACK

1 ounce reduced-fat cheddar cheese cubes with chilled steamed asparagus spears

LUNCH

Garden White Bean Soup (page 46)

Pulled Turkey Sandwich (page 131) without the bun

Chopped vegetable salad with Dijon vinaigrette

MIDAFTERNOON SNACK

Crudités with yogurt-scallion dip (made with nonfat or low-fat Greek-style plain yogurt and chopped scallions)

DINNER

Moroccan Spice-Rubbed Pork Chop (page 165)

Grilled Asparagus with Lemon Aioli (page 76)

Baby Greens with Tiny Tomatoes, Fresh Herbs, and Toasted Pistachios (page 74)

DESSERT

No-sugar-added Fudgsicle with an 8-ounce glass of 1% or fat-free milk

DAY 5

BREAKFAST

6 ounces tomato juice

Eggs Florentine (1 poached egg served on ½ cup spinach sautéed in extra-virgin olive oil)

2 low-fat turkey sausages

Coffee or tea with 1% or fat-free milk and sugar substitute

MIDMORNING SNACK

4 ounces 1% cottage cheese with chopped cucumbers

LUNCH

Curried Summer Squash Soup (page 36)

Seafood Caesar (page 63)

Hibiscus Tea Spritzer with Lime (page 231)

MIDAFTERNOON SNACK

Lettuce wrap with fat-free ham and a slice of reduced-fat Swiss cheese

DINNER

Pan-Seared Chicken with Roasted Tomatillo Salsa (page 140)

Grilled Eggplant Rounds with Garlicky Cilantro Topping (page 78)

Southern-Style Greens (page 85)

DESSERT

Iced Vanilla Coffee Milk (page 203) plus 15 almonds

DAY 6

BREAKFAST

6 ounces tomato juice

Silken tofu crumbled and scrambled with chives

2 slices Canadian bacon

Coffee or tea with 1% or fat-free milk and sugar substitute

MIDMORNING SNACK

Celery sticks with 2 tablespoons natural peanut butter

LUNCH

Lentil soup

Summer's Bounty Greek Salad (page 66)

MIDAFTERNOON SNACK

2 deviled egg halves

DINNER

Lemony Poached Halibut with Creamy Cucumbers (page 98)

Grilled Fennel with Mixed Olives (page 83)

Mesclun and cherry tomato salad with champagne vinaigrette

DESSERT

Creamy Lime-Vanilla Ricotta Soufflé (substitute lime for lemon in the recipe, page 197)

DAY 7

BREAKFAST

6 ounces tomato juice

Egg-white omelet with chopped Canadian bacon and mushrooms

Coffee or tea with 1% or fat-free milk and sugar substitute

MIDMORNING SNACK

Baba ghanoush with crudités

LUNCH

Heirloom Tomato Gazpacho (page 42)

Romaine Hearts with Tuna, Edamame, and Green Goddess Dressing (page 71)

MIDAFTERNOON SNACK

Endive spears topped with smoked trout

DINNER

Green and Yellow Beans with Fresh Mozzarella and Pine Nuts (page 62)

Indian Vegetable Curry (page 180)

DESSERT

Part-skim ricotta whisked with a dash of coconut extract and sugar substitute

HOW TO EAT ON PHASE 2

On the following pages, you'll find a week of sample meal plans for Phase 2. The key to continuing your weight loss on Phase 2 is to gradually reintroduce foods that were off-limits on Phase 1, so you can better monitor your hunger and possible cravings. For example, you can begin Phase 2 by having one whole-grain food and one fruit each day for the first few days in addition to your lean protein, vegetables, and low-fat dairy. If you continue to lose weight, you can gradually add more fruits, whole grains, and other foods. You will continue Phase 2 until you reach a weight that's healthy for you. Remember that this is a slower weight-loss phase than Phase 1: Losing 1 to 2 pounds a week on Phase 2 is excellent. (See page 3 for more information.)

The Day 1 meal plan gives you an idea of what you might eat on the first few days or weeks of Phase 2; the remainder of the meal plans illustrate days further into Phase 2, when you've added more fruit and other good carbohydrates. As with Phase 1, continue to eat plenty of vegetables, enjoy 2 to 3 cups of low-fat or nonfat dairy each day, and drink water.

A note about whole grains: On Phase 2, you will be introducing whole grains into your diet, but be sure you purchase the right ones. When you buy whole-grain breads and other products, be sure the label says "100% whole wheat" or "whole grain," not "enriched" or "fortified" grain or simply "100% wheat" or "multigrain." The process of refining white flour depletes it of much of its fiber and nutrients.

DAY 1

BREAKFAST

6 ounces tomato juice

Easy Walnut Muesli with Fresh Apricots (page 21)

2 slices Canadian bacon

Coffee or tea with 1% or fat-free milk and sugar substitute

MIDMORNING SNACK

Chopped hard-boiled egg with scallions and crumbled reduced-fat feta

LUNCH

Vegetable soup

Chipotle-Rubbed Steak Wrap (page 59)

MIDAFTERNOON SNACK

Hummus with red and yellow bell pepper strips

DINNER

Garlicky Chicken Skewers (page 129)

Steamed yellow beans with mint

Baked tomatoes with basil and Parmesan

DESSERT

Sugar-free chocolate pudding

DAY 2

BREAKFAST

6 ounces vegetable juice cocktail

Farmer's Cheese Pancakes with Summer Fruits (page 16)

Coffee or tea with 1% or fat-free milk and sugar substitute

MIDMORNING SNACK

Whole-wheat crackers with 1 ounce part-skim mozzarella cheese

LUNCH

Grilled Tuna with Provençal Anchovy Sauce (page 108)

Red leaf lettuce salad with shaved ricotta salata and herb vinaigrette

MIDAFTERNOON SNACK

¼ cup walnuts and an 8-ounce glass of 1% or fat-free milk

DINNER

Grilled Pork Tenderloin with Peach-Lime Salsa (page 150)

Moroccan Couscous (page 77)

Tossed salad (mixed greens, cucumbers, red and green bell peppers)

2 tablespoons low-sugar ranch dressing

DESSERT

South Beach Diet Tiramisu (page 196)

DAY 3

BREAKFAST

6 ounces tomato juice

Poached egg

Sweet Potato and Turkey Hash (page 24)

Coffee or tea with 1% or fat-free milk and sugar substitute

MIDMORNING SNACK

4 ounces 1% or fat-free cottage cheese with chives and radishes

LUNCH

Chilled consommé

South Beach Diet Club Sandwich (page 51)

Raspberry-Grape Sparkler (page 226)

MIDAFTERNOON SNACK

Reduced-fat Swiss cheese cubes with cherry tomatoes

DINNER

Steamed Mussels with Garden Vegetable Broth (page 115)

Grilled Shrimp Salad with Chile-Lime Dressing (page 124)

DESSERT

Chocolate-Cherry Truffles (page 200)

DAY 4

BREAKFAST

6 ounces vegetable juice cocktail

Greet-the-Sun Breakfast Pizza (page 23)

Coffee or tea with 1% or fat-free milk and sugar substitute

MIDMORNING SNACK

4 ounces nonfat or low-fat plain yogurt with ¾ cup fresh berries

LUNCH

Poached Chicken, Zucchini, and Wheat Berry Salad (page 65)

Orange Gingerade (page 217)

MIDAFTERNOON SNACK

1 part-skim mozzarella cheese stick

Cucumber and jícama slices

DINNER

Beef Satay with Peanut Sauce (page 149)

Summertime Sweet Potato Salad (page 81)

Citrusy Hot Pepper Slaw (page 93)

DESSERT

Strawberry-Blueberry Crunch (page 209) with an 8-ounce glass of 1% or fat-free milk

DAY 5

BREAKFAST

½ pink or red grapefruit

1 egg, any style

1 slice 100% whole-wheat toast with 1% cottage cheese, cinnamon, and a sprinkling of sugar substitute

Coffee or tea with 1% or fat-free milk and sugar substitute

MIDMORNING SNACK

1 medium pear with 1 ounce reduced-fat cheddar cheese

LUNCH

Spicy Chicken and Black Bean Taco (page 137)

Spinach salad with walnuts and lemon vinaigrette

MIDAFTERNOON SNACK

4 ounces low-fat or nonfat plain yogurt with almond extract and sugar substitute

DINNER

Warm Shrimp and Penne with Dill (page 104)

Sautéed Swiss chard with shallots

Boston lettuce salad with sliced sweet onions, kalamata olives, and 2 tablespoons low-sugar blue cheese dressing

DESSERT

Fresh Blackberry Tartlets (page 206)

DAY 6

BREAKFAST

6 ounces vegetable juice cocktail

Three Berry–Stuffed French Toast (page 29)

Coffee or tea with 1% or fat-free milk and sugar substitute

MIDMORNING SNACK

Vegetable dippers with Cucumber-Mint Yogurt (page 169)

LUNCH

Chilled Roasted Red and Yellow Pepper Soup with Avocado Salsa (page 34)

Middle Eastern Steak and Chickpea Salad (page 161)

Red leaf lettuce salad with sugar-free balsamic vinaigrette

MIDAFTERNOON SNACK

Chilled shrimp cocktail with zesty tomato-horseradish sauce

DINNER

Herb-Marinated Sirloin with Roasted Asparagus and Tomatoes (page 153)

Picnic Macaroni Salad (page 80)

Caesar salad (without croutons)

DESSERT

Nectarine and Plum Fans with Blue Cheese and Toasted Hazelnuts (page 198)

DAY 7

BREAKFAST

6 ounces tomato juice

Smoked Salmon and Cream Cheese "Breakwich" (page 31)

Coffee or tea with 1% or fat-free milk and sugar substitute

MIDMORNING SNACK

Mango Lassi (page 218)

LUNCH

Indian Spiced Chilled Tomato Soup (page 35)

Grilled Roasted Pepper, Red Onion, and Mozzarella Pizza (page 177)

Arugula salad with fresh lemon juice, black pepper, and olive oil

MIDAFTERNOON SNACK

½ cup dry-roasted edamame

DINNER

Pork Pinchos with Shredded Cabbage Salad (page 160)

Spicy Grilled Sweet Potato Fries (page 86)

Sliced garden tomatoes with fresh basil

DESSERT

Peach-Almond Parfait (page 211)

GLOSSARY OF INGREDIENTS

This selected list features many of the ingredients used in this book and will help you in preparing the healthy and delicious recipes.

APRICOTS: These soft-fleshed fruits are a good source of beta-carotene, vitamin C, fiber, potassium, and iron. They are available fresh in late spring and summer and dried year-round; use them to sweeten Easy Walnut Muesli (page 21).

ARUGULA: An Italian salad green with a peppery flavor, arugula is delicious in salads, sandwiches, and pasta dishes. We use it for Grilled Tomato, Arugula, and Feta Cheese Pizzas (page 175).

ASPARAGUS: A fiber-rich source of beta-carotene, vitamin C, and iron, asparagus is available fresh year-round in most supermarkets. Grill it for a side dish as we do (see page 76) or chop it for adding to pastas and salads.

AVOCADO: Mild with a smooth, buttery texture, avocados provide vitamin C and folate, along with healthy monounsaturated fat. Because avocados are high in calories, you'll want to limit your daily intake to one-third of a whole avocado.

BACON: Use turkey or Canadian bacon; both have the smoky taste you love from regular bacon, with less saturated fat. We add turkey bacon to our Southern-Style Greens (page 85) and Canadian bacon to the South Beach Diet Club Sandwiches (page 51).

BANANAS: High in vitamin B_6, bananas also provide pectin, a soluble fiber that may help lower cholesterol. Try them in our Blackberry-Banana Breakfast Smoothies (page 27) and our Floating Caribbean Islands dessert (page 208).

BEANS AND LEGUMES: A good source of protein and fiber, beans and other legumes are widely available both canned and dried. The following beans are used in this book:

- **Black beans:** Also known as Mexican, Spanish, or black turtle beans, black beans are an excellent source of iron, magnesium, phosphorus, and folate. Try them in Spicy Chicken and Black Bean Tacos (page 137).

- **Cannellini beans:** These white Italian beans (also called white kidney beans) have a nutty flavor and creamy texture. You'll love them in bean salads and minestrone soups; use them instead of Great Northern beans, if you like.

- **Chickpeas** (or garbanzo beans): These legumes have a mild nutty flavor and a firm yet creamy texture. Packed with protein, fiber, folate, iron, and zinc, they're perfect in our Mediterranean Vegetable Sandwiches (page 53) and Middle Eastern Steak and Chickpea Salad (page 161).

- **Edamame:** The Japanese word for soybeans, edamame come shelled and frozen, making it easy to drop a handful into soups, salads, and bean purées. Try them in Romaine Hearts with Tuna, Edamame, and Green Goddess Dressing (page 71).

- **Great Northern:** This white kidney-shaped bean can be used in any recipe calling for white beans, such as Garden White Bean Soup (page 46) or Easy Summer Chicken Chili (page 145).

- **Kidney beans:** This dark red bean is kidney shaped (thus its name). Its full-bodied flavor makes it a particularly good choice for chili and Red Beans and Rice (page 92). White kidney beans are known as cannellini (see above).

- **Soybeans:** See EDAMAME.

- **White beans:** See CANNELLINI and GREAT NORTHERN.

BEEF: A great source of iron, zinc, vitamin B$_{12}$, and protein, beef is also delicious and easy to cook. But not all cuts are equal when it comes to fat. Look for lean cuts like flank steak, London broil, tenderloin (filet mignon), T-bone, top round, bottom round, eye of round, sirloin, and top loin; veal chops and cutlets are also fine, as are bison and beefalo. Avoid porterhouse, rib roast, rib steak, and brisket, which are high in fat. Trim any visible fat before cooking. When choosing ground beef, look for extra lean, lean, or sirloin. Purchase natural grass-fed beef when possible.

BLACKBERRIES: A great source of the antioxidant vitamin C, blackberries also offer folate, iron, and pectin (a soluble fiber that may help to reduce cholesterol levels). Snack on these plump berries or use them as we do in smoothies, as a filling for French toast, and in desserts.

BLUEBERRIES: Available fresh or frozen, blueberries are a good source of disease-fighting antioxidants and fiber. They're delicious in our Blueberry-Almond Bran Muffins (page 20) and Summer Fruit Cocktail (page 212).

BRAN: A great source of fiber and magnesium, bran is the nutritious outer covering of wheat grains. Use it in Blueberry-Almond Bran Muffins (page 20).

BREAD: Choose 100% whole-wheat or whole-grain bread (try oat and bran, rye, sprouted grain, buckwheat, or other similar types) containing at least 3 grams of dietary fiber per slice for Phases 2 and 3. Bread is off-limits on Phase 1.

BROCCOLI: A nutritional powerhouse, fiber-rich broccoli is packed with folate, riboflavin, potassium, iron, and vitamin C. We use broccoli in our Vietnamese-Style Vegetables with Rice Noodles (page 187).

BROWN RICE: This wholesome rice is rich in thiamin, niacin, vitamin B$_6$, and fiber. When it comes to saving time, parboiled or precooked brown rice is a lifesaver—just make sure to purchase quick-cooking whole-grain brands that do not include partially hydrogenated oils.

CABBAGE: This crunchy crucifer is rich in vitamin C, fiber, and folate. Look for not only the common green and red cabbage but also Napa (which resembles romaine lettuce in shape and has a milder flavor than green or red cabbage) and Savoy (which resembles green but has frillier leaves and a stronger flavor).

CAPERS: Tiny, tangy, and slightly salty, these sun-dried flower buds make delicious sauces for chicken, meat, pasta, fish, and shellfish dishes (see Crab and Shrimp Cakes with Caper Sauce on page 101). Rinse them before using.

CARROTS: Available year-round, carrots are sweet and very high in beta-carotene. Reintroduce them to your diet on Phase 2.

CAULIFLOWER: A member of the cabbage family, cauliflower contains beneficial phytochemicals and also provides fiber, folate, and vitamin C. We add it to Indian Vegetable Curry (page 180).

CHEESE: A great source of calcium and protein, cheese can be high in saturated fat and calories. Choose low- or reduced-fat varieties that contain no more than 6 grams of fat per serving. The following types of cheese are used in this book:

- **Blue:** This type of cheese has been treated with molds that form the blue or green veins throughout and give the cheese its characteristic flavor. It does not come in reduced-fat versions, so use it modestly. Examples include Roquefort, Gorgonzola, and Stilton.

- **Cheddar:** This firm cow's milk cheese is available in a range of flavors from mild to sharp. Use the reduced-fat variety.

- **Cream cheese:** Low- and reduced-fat varieties of cream cheese make great spreads as well as omelet and cheesecake fillings. Try it in our Smoked Salmon and Cream Cheese "Breakwiches" (page 31).

- **Farmer's cheese:** This fresh cheese is a form of cottage cheese with the liquid pressed out. We use semisoft farmer's cheese in our Farmer's Cheese Pancakes with Summer Fruits (page 16) and Three Berry–Stuffed French Toast (page 29). You can also buy farmer's cheese in a solid loaf.

- **Feta:** Crumble this tangy Greek cheese into salads, like our Summer's Bounty Greek Salad (page 66), or onto pizza (page 175). Be sure to buy the reduced-fat variety.

- **Goat cheese:** Also called chèvre, goat cheese has a delicious flavor. In this book, we use the reduced-fat variety to liven up pasta (see page 191) and pizza (see page 176). It's also a great snack, spread on whole-grain crackers.

- **Monterey Jack:** This ivory-colored cow's milk cheese is great for melting and for sandwiches. Look for the reduced-fat version and try pepper Jack when you want an extra kick!

- **Mozzarella:** This mild cheese is delicious in salads and sandwiches and on pastas and pizzas. Choose the part-skim version.

- **Parmesan:** This nutty-tasting hard cheese is at its best when freshly grated. Since Parmesan is so versatile and full-flavored, we use it often. It does, however, have just over 8 grams of fat per ounce, so you'll want to use less than 1 ounce per serving (up to 3 tablespoons grated).

- **Ricotta:** This smooth cheese resembles cottage cheese but is sweeter-tasting and has four times more calcium. Try it in pastas like our Spaghetti with Ricotta and Fresh Tomato Sauce (page 173) and in desserts like South Beach Diet Tiramisu (page 196). Look for part-skim ricotta, which has all the flavor of the whole-milk version but 40 percent less fat.

- **Ricotta salata:** This is ricotta that's been aged at least 3 months, at which point it becomes a smooth, firm cheese suitable for shaving or grating. Try it in our Honeydew, Fresh Herb, and Ricotta Salata Salad (page 69).

CHERRIES: Cherries are a great source of vitamin C. Though fresh ones are available only in the summer months, you'll find frozen cherries year-round. You can use either kind in our Chocolate-Cherry Truffles (page 200).

CHILE PEPPERS: Chiles, which are high in vitamin C and beta-carotene, make great flavor boosters for all kinds of dishes. Look for fresh, canned, or jarred jalapeños in most large supermarkets. See also CHIPOTLES IN ADOBO and PEPPERONCINI.

CHILI PASTE: This spicy red paste, often flavored with garlic, can be found in the Asian foods section of large supermarkets. Use it in dishes like our Vietnamese Vegetables with Rice Noodles (page 187).

CHIPOTLES IN ADOBO: These smoked, dried red jalapeño chiles come in cans and are packed in a dark red sauce made from vinegar and other seasonings. Both the peppers and the sauce add punch to chili and other dishes. We use them for our Chipotle Chili Dogs (page 152) and Chipotle-Rubbed Steak Wraps (page 59).

CHOCOLATE: If you are on Phase 2 or 3 of the South Beach Diet, chocolate is allowed in moderation. Look for dark chocolate containing at least 70 percent cocoa to reap the heart-health benefits. We use bittersweet chocolate in our Chocolate-Cherry Truffles (page 200).

COCOA POWDER: Keep unsweetened cocoa powder on hand to make desserts like South Beach Diet Tiramisu (page 196) and Chocolate-Cherry Truffles (page 200).

COFFEE: Enjoy coffee on all phases of the South Beach Diet. Just limit caffeinated to 2 cups a day. We use it in our Iced Vanilla Coffee Milk dessert (page 203).

COOKING SPRAY, FAT-FREE: Use fat-free cooking spray on an outdoor grill grate, grill basket, or grill pan, or on a skillet to keep foods from sticking. To avoid flare-ups, always spray the grill or grill pan before heating. Fat-free cooking sprays are available in formulations devised especially for cooking at higher temperatures. Even those labeled olive oil or canola oil add no fat to your cooking because you use so little.

CORNICHONS: French for "gherkin," these tiny tart pickles are a delicious alternative to dill pickles in our Picnic Macaroni Salad (page 80) and Cool Cod Sandwiches with Homemade Tartar Sauce (page 57). See also PICKLES.

COUSCOUS: Made from semolina (coarsely ground durum wheat), couscous is a tasty alternative to rice and other grains. Purchase whole-wheat couscous, made from whole-grain durum flour; it contains the entire kernel of wheat, including the protein- and vitamin-rich endosperm and bran. Try Moroccan Couscous (page 77).

CUCUMBERS: You'll find countless uses for cucumbers in our recipes, from delicious salads to refreshing cold soups. Sliced cucumbers are a great base for dips or for a slice of reduced-fat cheese.

EGGPLANT: High in fiber, this globe-shaped vegetable is especially good grilled (page 78), added to kebabs (page 129), and with pasta (page 189). Look for Japanese or baby eggplants at specialty food stores.

EGGS: An economical source of protein, eggs are also packed with vitamin B_{12}, riboflavin, and selenium. Most South Beach Diet recipes use large eggs. Recent studies have shown moderate egg consumption to be safe and healthy. However, if you're concerned about your cholesterol, talk to your doctor and monitor your cholesterol while increasing egg consumption.

ENDIVE: There are many varieties of endive, including Belgian, curly, and escarole. In this book, we call for Belgian for our Endive Salad with Walnuts (page 67).

FARRO: This ancient relative of wheat has a hearty texture and a nutlike flavor. It is an excellent substitute for barley or whole-grain brown rice. We use it for our Grilled Salmon and Farro Salad (page 105).

FENNEL: This bulbous white vegetable is deliciously crisp and adds its bold anise-like flavor to salads as well as fish and meat dishes. When grilled, the flavor softens. Try it in Grilled Fennel with Mixed Olives (page 83).

FISH AND SHELLFISH: Fish is a good source of healthy protein. Since there are so many types, we can't provide information on all—but we do cover those that are used in this book. Because of mercury levels, it's best to limit consumption of canned albacore tuna (use light), swordfish, tilefish, and king mackerel.

- **Anchovies:** Anchovies are small saltwater fish of the herring family. They are sold in cans or jars and are a classic ingredient in a Caesar dressing. You can use mashed anchovies or anchovy paste (sold in tubes) for our Seafood Caesar (page 63). Use anchovies sparingly since they're high in sodium.

- **Clams:** You can find clams live in the shell, fresh or frozen shucked, or canned. These tasty shellfish are high in protein and offer fair amounts of calcium and iron. We call for fresh littlenecks for our Seafood Paella (page 100).

- **Cockles:** Traditionally more popular in Europe than in the United States, cockles are now available in many seafood markets. These tiny bivalves have a heart-shaped ribbed shell. Try them instead of littlenecks in Seafood Paella (page 100).

- **Cod:** This very tasty, lean white fish has a firm texture and a mild flavor. Try it in our Cool Cod Sandwiches with Homemade Tartar Sauce (page 57).

- **Crab:** Crabmeat is a good source of niacin, zinc, and omega-3 fatty acids. In this book, we call for fresh lump crabmeat, which consists of large choice chunks of body meat, for our Crab and Shrimp Cakes with Caper Sauce (page 101).

- **Halibut:** A flatfish like a flounder but much larger in size, mild-tasting halibut is commonly sold as fillets or steaks. Try our Lemony Poached Halibut with Creamy Cucumbers (page 98).

- **Lobster:** The king of shellfish, lobster is a good source of vitamin B_{12} and the antioxidant mineral selenium. While relatively high in cholesterol, lobster has only small amounts of artery-clogging saturated fat. Enjoy it in our Classic Lobster Rolls (page 54).

- **Monkfish:** Also called goosefish or anglerfish, firm-fleshed monkfish has a texture and flavor that is often compared to lobster. We combine it with shrimp for a delicious sandwich (page 56).

- **Mussels:** Low in fat, high in vitamin B_{12}, and rich in iron and selenium, mussels are easy to prepare. Steamed Mussels with Garden Vegetable Broth (page 115) will become a summertime favorite.

- **Salmon:** Thiamin, niacin, omega-3 fatty acids, potassium, and the vitamins B_6, B_{12}, and D are just a few of the healthful nutrients that this fish offers. Salmon is available fresh, smoked, and canned; it's so versatile, you'll find it in breakfast, lunch, and dinner recipes in this book.

- **Sea bass:** This firm-fleshed, mild-tasting fish is delicious grilled with a melon salsa (page 102). Avoid Chilean sea bass, which is overfished.

- **Shrimp:** This popular shellfish is widely available both fresh and frozen (and also peeled and deveined). Shrimp lend themselves to a variety of cooking techniques: sauté, grill, steam, or bake them. Remember, shrimp cook up in mere minutes; don't overcook them or they'll become tough and flavorless.

- **Spanish mackerel:** A relative of tuna, Spanish mackerel is rich in taste and in omega-3s, as well as B vitamins and the antioxidant selenium. If you've never tried Spanish mackerel, our Grilled Spanish Mackerel with Quick Pickled Onions (page 120) is a great place to start. Avoid king mackerel, which can be high in mercury.

- **Trout:** These freshwater fish have a mild, sweet flavor and are good broiled, grilled, or baked. Try our Lemon-Grilled Whole Trout with Pesto (page 113). Smoked trout makes a great snack.

- **Tuna:** An excellent source of B vitamins, tuna is rich in omega-3 fatty acids and the mineral selenium. Fresh tuna steaks are great for grilling (page 108) and can be ground for burgers (page 116). Canned light tuna is excellent for sandwiches (page 48) and salads (page 71). Avoid albacore, which can be high in mercury.

FISH SAUCE, ASIAN (*nam pla* or *nuoc nam*): This common Southeast Asian condiment made of fermented, salted fish is available in the Asian section of your supermarket or health-food store. We use it in our Vietnamese-Style Vegetables with Rice Noodles (page 187).

FLOUR: There are many nonwhite flours available for use in your baked and breakfast goods. We use whole-grain pastry flour for the baked goods in this book. This soft whole-wheat flour is better suited for light pastries, muffins, and cakes than denser, regular whole-wheat flour. If you can't find whole-grain pastry flour, you can use whole-wheat pastry flour instead. Occasionally we add a bit of white flour to Phase 3 baked goods (as in our Blueberry-Almond Bran Muffins on page 20) to give them a lighter texture.

GARLIC: Garlic is a key ingredient in many of the dishes in this book. Choose solid bulbs with tight skins. In general, 1 teaspoon of minced garlic is the equivalent of 1 whole garlic clove.

GRAPEFRUIT: All grapefruit provide vitamin C and fiber, but the pink and red varieties contain the powerful antioxidants beta-carotene and lycopene. As with oranges, to get the fiber, eat the whole fruit or, on Phase 3, drink the juice with pulp.

GRAPES: Naturally sweet and juicy, grapes make a good Phase 2 or 3 snack or dessert. You can also try them in our White Gazpacho (page 43) or in our Raspberry-Grape Sparklers (page 226), a great summer drink.

GREEN BEANS (AND YELLOW WAX BEANS): High in fiber, green and yellow beans also contain good amounts of beta-carotene and folate. We use both for Green and Yellow Beans with Fresh Mozzarella and Pine Nuts (page 62).

HALF-AND-HALF: Stick with fat-free half-and-half for baking or lightening your morning coffee (limit yourself to 1 tablespoon per cup). Better yet, try switching to 1% milk.

HERBS: Herbs are a must for cooking full-flavored dishes. In the summer, fresh herbs are particularly plentiful, but you can always use dried as a substitute. For more on herbs, see page 7.

- **Basil:** Fresh basil is used whole, torn, or chopped in salads, egg dishes, and pastas. Dried basil is perfect for baked chicken or fish and in soups. To make your own basil pesto, see page 13.

- **Chives:** A relative of onions and leeks, chives have a mild onion-like flavor. Snip them with scissors or gently chop them with a sharp knife, then try them in chicken salad or scrambled eggs.

- **Cilantro:** This lively tasting herb is delicious in salsas and salads or sprinkled over baked chicken or fish. To make cilantro pesto, see page 13.

- **Dill:** Available both fresh and dried, dill is a great addition to salads and sauces, as well as to fish, chicken, meat, and vegetable dishes.

- **Herbes de Provence:** Typically a mix of dried basil, fennel seed, lavender, marjoram, summer savory, rosemary, and thyme, this herb blend is found in the spice section of most supermarkets. In this book, we use it to flavor grilled tuna (page 108).

- **Marjoram:** A member of the mint family, marjoram has a sweet, oregano-like flavor. It can be found dried in the spice section of the supermarket. We use it as part of a rub for pan-grilled steak (page 153).

- **Mint:** There are more than 30 species of mint, but those most commonly sold in markets are peppermint and spearmint. We use mint often in this book to flavor salads, pasta, meat dishes, and drinks.

- **Parsley:** Fresh parsley makes a great garnish for cooked meats, chicken, and fish and is tasty in beans, pasta, and rice dishes. To make parsley pesto, see page 13.

- **Rosemary:** There's nothing quite like the piney flavor of this wonderful herb, which is often used to flavor meats, fish, soups, stews, vegetables, sauces, and dressings.

- **Sage:** This Mediterranean herb has a strong earthy flavor that is perfect for chicken, pork, ham, bean, and vegetable dishes.

- **Tarragon:** Distinguished by its anise-like flavor, tarragon is a great addition to fish and vegetable dishes and sauces.

- **Thyme:** Popular in French dishes, thyme has an assertive flavor that goes well with many foods, including tomato dishes and meats, poultry, and fish.

HORSERADISH: Enhance sauces, spreads, dressings, and sandwiches with convenient prepared horseradish. It comes jarred in the refrigerated section of the supermarket. We use it to make a zippy aioli for a vegetarian burger (page 188). You can also purchase this spicy member of the cabbage family fresh in the produce section and grate it yourself. See also WASABI.

HOT DOGS: Hot dogs (beef, pork, poultry, and soy) are a traditional part of summer cookouts. Just stick to products that are 97 percent fat free (3 to 6 grams of fat per serving) and enjoy them occasionally, no more than once a week. Go for whole-grain or whole-wheat buns, or eat the franks without a bun or with sauerkraut or our homemade tomato-pickle relish (page 158) and Dijon mustard. Check out our Chipotle Chili Dogs (page 152) and our Chicago-Style Grilled Tofu Dogs (page 181) for a change of pace.

HUMMUS: This thick Middle Eastern purée of chickpeas, garlic, fresh lemon juice, and olive oil makes a fantastic quick snack (with crudités or whole-grain crackers) and a great sandwich filling. It comes canned and fresh.

JÍCAMA: Also known as yam bean or Mexican turnip, jícama is a large bulbous root vegetable native to Central America. With a sweet nutty flavor that resembles a water chestnut, it is most often eaten raw in salads. Be sure to peel the thin outer skin before using it in our Crisp Jícama Salad with Creamy Cilantro Dressing (page 70).

KALE: This cruciferous cooking green is rich in fiber, vitamin C, vitamin B_6, and beta-carotene; it also provides calcium. It's delicious combined with turkey bacon, garlic, and onion in our Southern-Style Greens (page 85).

LAMB: Lamb is a fattier meat than many others. Buy a well-trimmed boneless leg, then have it ground for the kofta on page 156 or cubed for the kebabs on page 169.

LEMON: A fine source of vitamin C, this citrus fruit is a flavor enhancer for dressings, marinades, savory dishes, and desserts.

LIME: This vitamin C–rich citrus fruit lends terrific taste to all kinds of dishes, including our summery drinks.

MANGOES: An excellent source of beta-carotene, aromatic mangoes also provide soluble fiber and vitamin C. In this book, we use this tropical fruit in a shrimp dish (page 119), on a skewer (page 201), and for a refreshing drink (page 218).

MAYONNAISE: Used sparingly, mayonnaise makes delicious sandwich spreads and salad dressings. Purchase regular, reduced-fat, or dairy-free (soy-based, without eggs) mayonnaise. Avoid fat-free varieties and those made with high-fructose corn syrup.

MELONS: Good sources of potassium, vitamin C, and B vitamins, honeydew and cantaloupe are mildly sweet and extremely versatile. We use melons in a flavorful chilled soup (page 38) and a refreshing salad (page 69), as a dessert (page 208), and to make a slushy summer drink (page 232).

MILK: Milk is an important source of protein, calcium, and vitamins A, D, and B_{12}. Choose fat-free and 1% milk, which contain the same nutrients as whole milk but without the high amount of saturated fat. Enjoy it in our Iced Vanilla Coffee Milk (page 203).

MIRIN: Also referred to as rice wine, this low-alcohol cooking wine made from glutinous rice adds a sweet flavor to Japanese dishes. It can be found in the Asian section of most supermarkets. Make a substitute for mirin by adding 2 tablespoons of granular sugar substitute to 1 cup of dry white wine. Stir the mixture well and keep it refrigerated for up to 1 month.

MUSTARD: We use mustard liberally on the South Beach Diet because it's such a terrific and convenient flavor enhancer. Try regular or coarse-grained Dijon in our Seafood Caesar (page 63) and Savory Egg Salad Sandwiches (page 47). Avoid honey mustards or any others that contain sugar.

NECTARINES: A good source of potassium and fiber, these smooth-skinned, fuzzless relatives of the peach are at their peak in midsummer. Start the day with Whole-Grain Nectarine Pancakes (page 17).

NUTS: High in protein and fiber and very satisfying, nuts make a great snack and add wonderful crunch to salads and rice dishes. They also show up in extracts, desserts, and sauces and are used to make oils, butters, and flour. Remember to stick to recommended portion sizes, as nuts are high in calories. The following nuts are used in this book:

- **Almonds:** Rich in vitamin E, these heart-healthy nuts also contain riboflavin, iron, and magnesium. They're higher in fiber than most other nuts.

- **Hazelnuts:** Wonderfully sweet, hazelnuts are popular in savory dishes and desserts. They are a good source of monounsaturated fat, found to be helpful in lowering LDL ("bad") cholesterol levels.

- **Peanut butter:** High in monounsaturated fat, folate, and resveratrol (a phytochemical found in red wine that helps protect against heart disease and cancer), peanut butter is wonderful in dishes like Beef Satay with Peanut Sauce (page 149). You can enjoy it spread on celery for a healthy, portable, hunger-curbing snack on Phase 1. Limit peanut butter to 2 tablespoons per serving and purchase natural trans-fat-free and sugar-free varieties only.

- **Peanuts:** Though used and thought of as nuts, peanuts are actually legumes. They contain good amounts of vitamin E, folate, niacin, and magnesium. We use them in our Curried Chicken Salad with Peanuts (page 136).

- **Pine nuts:** Also known as pignoli or piñon, pine nuts are the seeds of certain pinecones. Delicious in salads, pastas, and baked goods, they keep best in an airtight container in the refrigerator or freezer.

- **Pistachios:** These nuts provide vitamin E, iron, thiamin, and magnesium. Sprinkle them over salads, chicken dishes, and desserts.

- **Walnuts:** Walnuts are unique in the nut world in that they contain alpha-linolenic acid (ALA), a polyunsaturated fatty acid related to the heart-protective omega-3s, along with many other nutrients. We use them in Easy Walnut Muesli with Fresh Apricots (page 21) and Endive Salad with Walnuts (page 67).

OATS: This flavor-packed grain offers 50 percent more protein than bulgur wheat and twice as much as brown rice. Oats are also impressively high in fiber and provide thiamin, iron, selenium, magnesium, and zinc. Choose rolled or steel-cut oats over instant-cook oatmeal (which is too highly processed). You'll enjoy oats in our muesli (page 21).

OILS: Oils are extremely important ingredients, especially in South Beach Diet recipes, where you'll use them to sauté, and for sauces, salad dressings, and marinades. You'll want to store most oils in a cool, dark pantry (except for nut oils, which belong in the fridge). We use the following oils in this book:

- **Canola oil:** This bland-tasting oil comes from the seeds of the same plant that gives us the vegetable broccoli rabe. The oil is rich in alpha-linolenic acid (ALA), a heart-protective polyunsaturated fatty acid. Canola oil is perfect for sautéing and for salad dressings.

- **Extra-virgin olive oil:** Made from the first pressing of the olives, this oil has a low acid content and a delicate flavor and is a good source of anti-inflammatory monounsaturated fat. Extra-virgin olive oil can be used for cooking, making salad dressings, or simply drizzling over fresh vegetables.

• **Sesame oil:** This full-flavored Asian oil is made from sesame seeds and comes in cold-pressed and toasted forms. We use toasted sesame oil in our Asian Tuna Burgers (page 116) and Savoy Slaw with Sesame Dressing (page 88). Look for it in the Asian section of most supermarkets and store it in a cool, dry place.

OLIVES: These small, flavor-packed fruits make a fantastic snack, appetizer, and salad ingredient; they also taste great in pastas as well as meat and fish dishes. Olives contain healthy monounsaturated fatty acids, which may help to lower "bad" LDL cholesterol. Stick to recommended portion sizes because they are high in calories.

ONIONS: Keep onions (including red, white, Spanish or yellow, sweet Vidalia, shallots, and scallions) on hand; you'll find them in many South Beach Diet recipes because they are great flavor enhancers.

ORANGES: Good sources of vitamin C, folate, and fiber, oranges make a refreshing portable snack on Phases 2 and 3 and are a nice addition to salads and drinks. To get the maximum fiber, eat the whole fruit or, on Phase 3, drink the juice with pulp.

PANCAKE SYRUP, SUGAR-FREE: Suitable for whole-grain pancakes (which you can enjoy on Phases 2 and 3), this syrup also gives extra flavor to our tasty Pulled Turkey Sandwiches (page 131) and Tempeh and Vegetable Fajitas (page 193).

PAPAYAS: These tropical fruits, which range in color from all-yellow to yellow-green, are a good source of vitamins C and E. Avoid completely green papayas, which are not ripe. The flesh of a ripe papaya will give slightly when gently pressed.

PASTA: Use whole-wheat or spelt pastas, which are flavorful, nutrient and fiber rich, and readily available in the health-food section of large supermarkets.

PEACHES: Peaches are classified as either freestone (the flesh slips easily off the pit) or clingstone. Freestone peaches are softer and juicier than clingstone and best for the recipes in this book. Enjoy them in our Farmer's Cheese Pancakes with Summer Fruits (page 16) and our Peach-Raspberry Shakes (page 230).

PEAS: Available fresh and frozen, peas are sweet and tasty, low in fat, and high in fiber. Reintroduce them on Phase 2. See also SNOW PEAS, which are allowed on Phase 1.

PEPPERONCINI: Also known as Tuscan peppers or sweet Italian peppers, these pickled peppers are widely available jarred and range from mild to medium-hot.

PEPPERS, BELL: A good source of beta-carotene and vitamin C, sweet peppers provide fiber and add delicious flavor to many dishes. Jarred, roasted red peppers are widely available and are a key ingredient when it comes to convenience. See also CHILE PEPPERS and PEPPERONCINI.

PESTO: This blend of fresh basil, pine nuts, Parmesan cheese, and olive oil is delicious tossed with pasta or drizzled over meats and fish. You can even mix it with reduced-fat sour cream for a tasty dip. Store-bought pesto is widely available, but you can easily make your own when basil is at its summer peak (see page 13).

PHYLLO: The Greek word for "leaf," phyllo is a tissue-thin dough used in Greek dishes. We use it for our Fresh Blackberry Tartlets (page 206). You'll find mini phyllo tart shells in the freezer section of supermarkets and health-food stores.

PICKLES: Pickles make a tangy and delicious side dish at barbecues and picnics. If you are watching your sodium, use only moderate amounts. No-sugar-added pickles and pickle relishes are available in many supermarkets. You can also make your own pickle relish (page 158). Increase the quantity as desired. See also CORNICHONS.

PLUMS: There are more than 140 varieties of this colorful fruit, ranging from green to purple to blue. Experiment with different kinds for the recipes in this book or use them instead of peaches or nectarines, if you prefer.

POMEGRANATE: This late-fall and winter fruit bears delicious seeds and also offers an impressive and concentrated source of antioxidants as well as vitamin B_6 and potassium. In summer, use 100% pomegranate juice, available at most supermarkets, for making our Iced Pom-Mojito Spritzers (page 228).

PORK: Lean cuts of pork (chops, cutlets, loin, and tenderloin) are tasty forms of protein. Though you should stay away from regular bacon and hams cured with honey, you can eat moderate amounts of Canadian bacon and fat-free or low-fat boiled ham.

POULTRY: Choose skinless chicken breasts, turkey breasts, or chicken cutlets, which are high in protein and low in fat. Turkey bacon and reduced-fat turkey sausages are fine, but avoid duck and goose, as well as dark-meat chicken and turkey (legs and wings), since these are high in fat. Also avoid processed poultry nuggets and patties. Purchase antibiotic- and hormone-free chicken and turkey when possible.

RADISHES: These crisp and crunchy root vegetables are high in potassium and vitamin C. Try them sliced in our Grilled Southwest Steak, Radish, and Blue Cheese Salad (page 72) or on their own as a snack.

RASPBERRIES: A good source of fiber, raspberries also contain antioxidant vitamins, including vitamin C. Raspberries are available fresh or frozen (avoid frozen versions that contain added sugar); you can also freeze your own (see page 10).

RICE: See BROWN RICE.

RICE NOODLES: Dried Asian rice noodles are usually sold coiled in bags. They come in thin or wide varieties. The thinner form is sold as rice vermicelli; the wider form is called rice sticks. We use the wider type in our Vietnamese Vegetables with Rice Noodles (page 187).

RICE VINEGAR: See VINEGAR.

RICE WINE: See MIRIN.

SALAD DRESSING: In this book, we offer many easy, healthy salad dressings using extra-virgin olive oil and vinegar or fresh lemon or lime juice. They are featured with the salad recipes (not in a dressing and condiment section). Use any of these dressings for your favorite salads or purchase low-sugar varieties that contain no more than 3 grams of sugar per serving. Remember to steer clear of low-fat salad dressings, which are often high in sugars and unhealthy processed ingredients.

SALSA: This mix of chopped tomatoes, onions, chiles, and cilantro comes canned, jarred (avoid high-sugar, high-sodium varieties), but you can easily make your own. Avocado salsa makes a fine addition to our Chilled Roasted Red and Yellow Pepper Soup (page 34).

SAUSAGES: Look for lean turkey (the leanest) or chicken sausages in mild and hot varieties. You'll want to read labels carefully to avoid fillers, like sugars, fats, and bread crumbs.

SEEDS: Because seeds are high in calories, limit your intake to about 1 ounce, or ¼ cup, a day. Seeds are also used to make OILS. The following seeds are used in this book:

- **Flaxseeds:** Flaxseeds, sold ground and whole, are a good source of alpha–linolenic acid (ALA), which promotes the health of cell membranes, including those of the heart. Flaxseed is also high in fiber and helps keep your digestive system healthy. We use it as a topping for muesli (page 21).

- **Pumpkin seeds:** Pumpkin seeds are rich in vitamin E, iron, magnesium, and zinc, and they also provide essential and nonessential fatty acids. They are sold in the shell, shelled, roasted, and raw in health-food stores and better supermarkets. Try them in Spanish Rice Salad with Pumpkin Seeds (page 89).

- **Sesame seeds:** These tiny oval seeds come hulled and unhulled. The unhulled type, which are darker in color, have the bran intact and are an excellent source of iron and phosphorus. Try them in Asian Tuna Burgers (page 116).

- **Sunflower seeds:** Sunflower seeds, which enhance our muesli (page 21), are an excellent source of the antioxidant vitamin E, as well as folate, iron, manganese, and selenium.

SHALLOTS: Shallots have a flavor somewhere in between onion and garlic. They are available in both yellow and red varieties. Shallot heads have multiple cloves covered in a thin papery skin, which is easily removed. See also ONIONS.

SNOW PEAS: These completely edible pea pods, fine on Phase 1, are light green with small immature-looking peas inside (they are picked before the seeds have fully developed). Snow peas have more than three times the amount of vitamin C of green peas, as well as vitamin E, folate, lutein, and zeaxanthin. Snow peas can be served raw in salads, but blanching them for a minute brings out their color.

SOY SAUCE: Made from fermented soybeans, wheat, water, and salt, soy sauce can be used to flavor poultry, fish, and meat, as well as vegetables, sauces, soups, and marinades. Lower-sodium versions are available.

SPICES: These aromatic seasonings come from the bark, buds, fruit, roots, seeds, or stems of plants and trees. Generally, all spices that don't contain added sugar are recommended on the South Beach Diet. Using them in your cooking is an easy—and quick—way to add more flavor to food. Buy spices ground or whole and store them in a cool, dark place for up to 6 months. Those listed below are used in this book. Feel free to use your own favorites if you don't see them listed here.

- **Cajun seasoning:** Cajun seasoning blends typically contain salt, cayenne, paprika, black and white pepper, and onion and garlic powder.

- **Cayenne:** This spicy seasoning, made from ground dried cayenne chile peppers, works well in meat and fish dishes, as well as chili and spicy soups.

- **Chili powder:** Chili powder generally refers to a blend that contains ground chile peppers, cumin, garlic powder, and salt. You'll also find pure chile powders (like ancho chile powder), which will be labeled as such.

- **Cinnamon:** This bittersweet spice is wonderful in baked goods and also makes appearances in savory dishes (especially in Greek and Moroccan cuisines).

- **Crab boil seasoning:** There are many versions of this available, but it typically contains bay leaf, celery salt, mustard seed, nutmeg, cloves, paprika, and other spices.

- **Cumin:** Common in Mexican, Indian, and Tex-Mex cooking, cumin is a heady spice with an aromatic scent. It is delicious in meat and vegetable dishes.

- **Curry powder:** Used widely in Indian cooking, this blend of many spices (including cardamon, cumin, and coriander) ranges from mild to hot.

- **Ginger:** Wonderful in desserts as well as savory dishes, this warming, piquant spice is available fresh and ground.

- **Jerk seasoning:** This blend of herbs and spices, often used in Jamaican cooking, is rubbed onto meats, poultry, or fish before cooking. It typically includes chiles, thyme, cinnamon, ginger, cloves, and garlic. Make your own (page 11).

- **Nutmeg:** Another sweet spice, nutmeg is sold whole and ground. For best flavor, grate or grind the nutmeg yourself.

- **Paprika:** A dried version of mild to hot peppers, this spice lends flavor and color to savory dishes. You'll find sweet, bittersweet, hot, and smoked paprika.

- **Pepper:** This popular spice comes whole and ground in black, white, green, and pink varieties. Grind whole peppercorns as you need them for the freshest taste.

- **Red pepper flakes:** Great for sprinkling onto pasta, pizza, and other Italian dishes, red pepper flakes are also used to spice up savory Asian dishes.

SQUASH, SUMMER: More than 95 percent water, summer squash have modest amounts of vitamin C, fiber, potassium, and magnesium. Popular varieties include zucchini, yellow straightneck, yellow crookneck, and pattypan. The edible skin contains healthy carotenoids, so don't peel squash unless a recipe calls for doing so.

STRAWBERRIES: High in vitamin C and fiber, these sweet berries make a great breakfast or Phase 2 or 3 snack and are delicious in desserts (like our Strawberry-Blueberry Crunch on page 209). Buy them fresh in season or frozen year-round.

SUGAR: Try to avoid white sugar when following the South Beach Diet. However, a small amount of regular sugar may be introduced on Phase 3 as an ingredient in baked goods for an occasional treat. Remember to monitor yourself for the return of cravings if you do eat sugar.

SUGAR SUBSTITUTE: Use any of the following no-calorie sweeteners: aspartame (NutraSweet, Equal), sucralose (Splenda), saccharin (Sprinkle Sweet, Sweet'N Low), or acesulfame K (Sweet One). Some sugar substitutes may be made with sugar alcohols (isomalt, lacitol, mannitol, sorbitol, or xylitol) and are permitted on the South Beach Diet. They may have associated side effects of gastrointestinal distress if consumed in excess.

SUN-DRIED TOMATOES: Usually packed in oil, these tangy treats enhance sauces, soups, and salads. Buy a low-sodium brand, if you can find it.

SWEET POTATO: This remarkable vegetable is high in fiber and rich in beta-carotene, vitamin B_6, vitamin C, iron, and potassium. Try our Spicy Grilled Sweet Potato Fries (page 86).

TAPENADE: A thick paste usually made from olives, olive oil, lemon juice, capers, anchovies, and seasonings, tapenade is used in our Tofu Salad Sandwiches with Tapenade (page 185), but it's also great on fish and poultry. Look for jarred varieties with no sugar added.

TEA: Tea is not just a morning drink; it also makes a refreshing iced drink on a hot summer day—try our Iced Green Sun Tea (page 225) and our Hibiscus Tea Spritzers with Lime (page 231). Limit caffeinated teas to 2 cups per day.

TEMPEH: Available fresh or frozen, tempeh is made from fermented soybeans formed into a nutty-tasting cake. Frozen tempeh keeps well for several months; thawed, it will keep in the refrigerator for about 10 days. Since it's fermented like cheese, tempeh may develop some harmless mold on the surface. Simply cut it away.

TOFU: Made from soymilk curd, which is pressed into small blocks, tofu is rich in iron and is also a good source of protein. Tofu comes in silken and regular varieties, which in turn are characterized as soft, firm, and extra firm. Silken tofu is smoother and generally better for baking or smoothies; regular is more granular in texture. Firm and extra firm are best for stir-fries and omelets.

TOMATILLOS: Also known as Mexican tomatoes, tomatillos look like small green tomatoes with papery husks. Tangy and slightly lemony and herbaceous, their pronounced flavor softens when they are cooked. Look for firm specimens, with tight-fitting husks. When ready to cook, simply remove the papery covering with your fingers; the naturally sticky coating underneath will wash off with water.

TOMATOES: A height-of-summer treat, fresh tomatoes come in numerous varieties from beefsteaks and heirlooms to tiny cherry, grape, and currant types. They provide fiber, B vitamins, iron, potassium, and vitamin C, as well as the carotenoid lycopene, which has been shown to help reduce the risk of prostate cancer and cardiovascular disease. Tomatoes also come canned and in sun-dried form (see SUN-DRIED TOMATOES). Canned varieties include stewed, diced, whole, crushed, and Italian and Mexican diced. Avoid brands that are high in sugar.

TORTILLAS: Sometimes sold as wraps, whole-wheat tortillas are delicious and healthful in our Barbecued Tofu Wraps (page 192), Grilled Fish Tacos with Spicy Melon Salsa (page 102), and more.

TRANS-FAT-FREE MARGARINE (or light and reduced-fat spreads): Sold in tubs, trans-fat-free margarine and spreads are a heart-healthy alternative to stick margarine and butter. Some spreads also contain plant sterols and stanols, which have been found to help reduce cholesterol. As with any fat, use these products in moderation.

TURKEY: Roasted turkey breast, plain or smoked, is available in most delis. We cube the breast for our Sweet Potato and Turkey Hash (page 24) and poach it and "pull" it for Pulled Turkey Sandwiches (page 131). You can also ask for extra-thin salt-free or reduced-sodium slices and use them to make sandwiches like our South Beach Diet Club Sandwiches (page 51). Turkey hot dogs, turkey bacon, and turkey sausage are also available.

VINEGAR: Vinegar adds a bright, jazzy flavor to marinades and quick dressings. Among the most popular varieties are balsamic, champagne, cider vinegar, rice vinegar, and red and white wine vinegar. You can also purchase herb- and garlic-flavored vinegars or make your own herb vinegar (see page 7). Look for rice vinegar, made from fermented rice, in the Asian section of large supermarkets or, for the highest quality, in Asian liquor stores.

WASABI: Also known as Japanese horseradish, this spicy green paste typically accompanies sushi and sashimi in Japanese restaurants. It is sold as a powder to be reconstituted with a little water, or as a paste. Most supermarkets carry it.

WHEAT BERRIES: Also called groats, wheat berries are wheat kernels that have not been milled, polished, or heat treated. The hard variety can take more than an hour to cook unless presoaked overnight; the soft variety, which we use in our Poached Chicken, Zucchini, and Wheat Berry Salad (page 65), needs only brief soaking.

YOGURT: High in calcium, yogurt also provides protein, B vitamins, and minerals. On Phase 1, enjoy nonfat or low-fat plain yogurt. In later phases, you can incorporate artificially sweetened, fat-free flavored yogurts as long as you avoid products that contain high-fructose corn syrup. We also recommend nonfat or low-fat Greek-style yogurt, which is strained before it is packaged to produce a creamy product. Try it in our Sweet Strawberries with Greek-Style Yogurt and Almonds (page 18).

INDEX

Underscored page references indicate sidebars. **Boldface** references indicate photographs.

Conversion Chart

These equivalents have been slightly rounded to make measuring easier.

Volume Measurements

U.S.	Imperial	Metric
¼ tsp	–	1 ml
½ tsp	–	2 ml
1 tsp	–	5 ml
1 Tbsp	–	15 ml
2 Tbsp (1 oz)	1 fl oz	30 ml
¼ cup (2 oz)	2 fl oz	60 ml
⅓ cup (3 oz)	3 fl oz	80 ml
½ cup (4 oz)	4 fl oz	120 ml
⅔ cup (5 oz)	5 fl oz	160 ml
¾ cup (6 oz)	6 fl oz	180 ml
1 cup (8 oz)	8 fl oz	240 ml

Weight Measurements

U.S.	Metric
1 oz	30 g
2 oz	60 g
4 oz (¼ lb)	115 g
5 oz (⅓ lb)	145 g
6 oz	170 g
7 oz	200 g
8 oz (½ lb)	230 g
10 oz	285 g
12 oz (¾ lb)	340 g
14 oz	400 g
16 oz (1 lb)	455 g
2.2 lb	1 kg

Length Measurements

U.S.	Metric
¼"	0.6 cm
½"	1.25 cm
1"	2.5 cm
2"	5 cm
4"	11 cm
6"	15 cm
8"	20 cm
10"	25 cm
12" (1')	30 cm

Pan Sizes

U.S.	Metric
8" cake pan	20 × 4 cm sandwich or cake tin
9" cake pan	23 × 3.5 cm sandwich or cake tin
11" × 7" baking pan	28 × 18 cm baking tin
13" × 9" baking pan	32.5 × 23 cm baking tin
15" × 10" baking pan	38 × 25.5 cm baking tin (Swiss roll tin)
1½ qt baking dish	1.5 liter baking dish
2 qt baking dish	2 liter baking dish
2 qt rectangular baking dish	30 × 19 cm baking dish
9" pie plate	22 × 4 or 23 × 4 cm pie plate
7" or 8" springform pan	18 or 20 cm springform or loose-bottom cake tin
9" × 5" loaf pan	23 × 13 cm or 2 lb narrow loaf tin or pâté tin

Temperatures

Fahrenheit	Centigrade	Gas
140°	60°	–
160°	70°	–
180°	80°	–
225°	105°	¼
250°	120°	½
275°	135°	1
300°	150°	2
325°	160°	3
350°	180°	4
375°	190°	5
400°	200°	6
425°	220°	7
450°	230°	8
475°	245°	9
500°	260°	–